The Princeton Review

Geography
Smart Junior

A Young Explorer's Guide to the World

BOOKS IN THE PRINCETON REVIEW SERIES

Cracking the ACT
Cracking the ACT with Sample Tests on CD-ROM
Cracking the CLEP (College-Level Examination Program)
Cracking the GED
Cracking the GMAT
Cracking the GMAT with Sample Tests on Computer Disk
Cracking the GRE
Cracking the GRE with Sample Tests on Computer Disk
Cracking the GRE Biology Subject Test
Cracking the GRE Literature in English Subject Test
Cracking the GRE Psychology Subject Test
Cracking the LSAT
Cracking the LSAT with Sample Tests on Computer Disk
Cracking the LSAT with Sample Tests on CD-ROM
Cracking the MAT (Miller Analogies Test)
Cracking the NTE with Audio CD-ROM
Cracking the SAT and PSAT
Cracking the SAT and PSAT with Sample Tests on
    Computer Disk
Cracking the SAT and PSAT with Sample Tests on CD-ROM
Cracking the SAT II: Biology Subject Test
Cracking the SAT II: Chemistry Subject Test
Cracking the SAT II: English Subject Tests
Cracking the SAT II: French Subject Test
Cracking the SAT II: History Subject Tests
Cracking the SAT II: Math Subject Tests
Cracking the SAT II: Physics Subject Test
Cracking the SAT II: Spanish Subject Test
Cracking the TOEFL with Audiocassette
Flowers & Silver MCAT
Flowers Annotated MCAT
Flowers Annotated MCATs with Sample Tests on
    Computer Disk
Flowers Annotated MCATs with Sample Tests on CD-ROM

Culturescope Grade School Edition
Culturescope High School Edition
Culturescope College Edition

LSAT/GRE Analytic Workout
SAT Math Workout
SAT Verbal Workout

All U Can Eat
Don't Be a Chump!
How to Survive Without Your Parents' Money
Speak Now!
Trashproof Resumes

Biology Smart
Grammar Smart
Math Smart
Reading Smart
Study Smart
Word Smart: Building an Educated Vocabulary
Word Smart II: How to Build a More Educated Vocabulary
Word Smart Executive
Word Smart Genius
Writing Smart

American History Smart Junior
Astronomy Smart Junior
Geography Smart Junior
Grammar Smart Junior
Math Smart Junior
Word Smart Junior
Writing Smart Junior

Business School Companion
College Companion
Law School Companion
Medical School Companion

Student Advantage Guide to College Admissions
Student Advantage Guide to the Best 310 Colleges
Student Advantage Guide to America's Top Internships
Student Advantage Guide to Business Schools
Student Advantage Guide to Law Schools
Student Advantage Guide to Medical Schools
Student Advantage Guide to Paying for College
Student Advantage Guide to Summer
Student Advantage Guide to Visiting College Campuses
Student Advantage Guide: Help Yourself
Student Advantage Guide: The Complete Book of Colleges
Student Advantage Guide: The Internship Bible
Hillel Guide to Jewish Life on Campus
International Students' Guide to the United States
The Princeton Review Guide to Your Career

Also available on cassette from Living Language
Grammar Smart
Word Smart
Word Smart II

The Princeton Review

Geography
Smart Junior

A Young Explorer's Guide to the World

by J. Allen Queen

Random House, Inc., New York 1997

Princeton Review Publishing, L.L.C.
2315 Broadway, 3rd Floor
New York, NY 10024
E-mail: web-info@review.com

ISBN 0-679-77522-6

Designed by: Illeny Maaza
Map illustrations by: Adam Hurwitz
Edited by: Bronwyn Collie

Manufactured in the United States of America on recycled paper.

9 8 7 6 5 4 3 2 1

Acknowledgments

Special thanks to Bronwyn Collie, Illeny Maaza, John Bergdahl, Adam Hurwitz, Kirsten Ulve, and The Princeton Review Staff for their sincere assistance and for making this book possible.

Dedicated to my wife, Patsy, and my son, Alex.
Thanks for all your guidance and support.

CONTENTS

Introduction

How many times in social studies class have you heard, "Get out your textbook, read chapter 4, and answer the questions at the back of the chapter?"

Does that make you want to %*^&^*&$&%*? Or, at least, take a long nap? Yes, that is a pretty boring way to learn. It's not that the information itself is boring, it's just that it's presented in an uninteresting manner.

What if you could learn about physical geography in an exciting way that is comical, gets you involved, and is something you can do with your friends? You might be interested, right? Well, you have it in your hands: *Geography Smart Junior* is a creative, interesting way to learn. Other than getting on a plane, ship, or train and experiencing geography first hand, reading this book, and doing the short quizzes and activities, will be one of the most exciting ways you'll learn about physical geography.

You'll travel and learn along with Bridget, Babette, Barnaby, and Beauregard, as they follow the clues that take them all around the world, and finally to the $20 million treasure to be donated to a worthy cause. By the time you've finished this book, you'll be an expert too. Use *Geography Smart Junior* to have fun as you learn. After all, learning should be an enjoyable experience.

Chapter 1

The Treasure of Bartholomew Van Morrow

Allow me to introduce myself. My name is Beauregard, and I am presently relaxing back home in South Carolina. For generations, my family has resided in some of the most aristocratic homes in the state. Indeed, my family knows what quality living is and, as you might expect, we long ago perfected feline manners and grace.

There is just one downside to the genteel life in South Carolina, and that is having to endure the hot, steamy summers (think, for example, of the amount of time one must spend grooming if one's fur is to look attractive despite the heat). Why, it is only early June now and, as I am lying here on the verandah, the blazing midday sun is already creeping up on my shady spot. Pardon me while I stretch a bit...

My adventures, as I prefer to call them, have allowed me to escape the South Carolina summers over the years. The first summer away resulted from a rowdy case of spring fever during my reckless youth when my family (who refer to my adventures as gallivanting) insisted I go to Paris until the gossip died down. You must understand that preserving the family reputation is very important among Southern aristocratic feline families. To be frank, it worked out rather nicely for me—I was only too pleased to be able to escape the intolerable heat. After that first summer in Paris, I spent many others globetrotting with interesting, colorful characters. Just lately, however, my summers have involved a little more work. You see, I had the "fortune" to meet three somewhat unusual young people, who have a tendency to get into *situations*. Being the sort of cat I am, I took it upon myself (some would say I am crazy) to keep an eye on them. Alas, being a cat of the world has its obligations as well as its privileges.

Ah yes, the adventures I have had with Bridget, Babette, and Barnaby! Thankfully, those are now behind me, and my current quest is simply to find a more shady spot on the verandah. Once found, I'll slink over to take the perfect afternoon nap. I'm beginning to suspect, however, that an entire summer of simply moving from one shady spot to another will become tiresome. Hmmm…maybe I should give some thought to paying my pal Luigi a visit in New York. He usually likes to flee the noisy, hot city during the summer when the only entertainment is sitting on a fence with the other tomcats watching the garbage pile up during a collectors' strike. That's a pretty smelly, not to mention unrefined, way to pass the time if you ask me. Yes, I could visit New York (and one or two beautiful acquaintances while I'm there) for a couple of days, then Luigi and I could head off somewhere cool for the summer.

✎ ✎ ✎ ✎ ✎

Bridget twisted her New York Yankees cap around on her head. She could still hear her teacher, Ms. Espisito, saying, "I hope you all enjoy a wonderful summer vacation!" "Yeah, right," thought Bridget as she plopped down in her overstuffed chair.

Bridget's mom had told her in March that the summer was likely to be very busy at her law firm, and that any vacation would be a short one at the end of August. To make matters worse, her mom was convinced by an old college friend to send Bridget to his summer camp in Maine for most of the summer. "Camp Novachuk," thought Bridget. "It ought to be called Camp Nerdachuk!"

Her mom's friend had bored her for hours when he came to dinner last April. His soup got cold, then his entree, then his dessert, as he droned on and on about chutes and ladders tournaments, horseshoe tournaments, and the endless techniques of lanyard construction that would be addressed in craft class. "I just don't see myself making that scene this summer," Bridget thought. "But how can I talk my mom out of it?"

She pondered the vision of spending two months going down chutes and up ladders, throwing horseshoes, and comparing lanyard techniques with her fellow campers as high points of the summer. In fact, it was enough to get her up out of the chair and through the front door with the resolve to visit her mother at the office in an effort to talk her out of this plan for a miserable summer....

Entering the law office that morning was like stepping into a Kansas twister. The normally quiet, staid office was full of lawyers, secretaries, and message delivery boys zipping around amid flying papers, ringing telephones, and shouting voices. "What bomb exploded?" thought Bridget as her eyes searched the chaos for her mother.

"Bridget," called her mother as she came out of her office carrying a stack of files. "What are you doing here?"

Bridget worked her way across to her mother and followed her into her office. "What's going on around here?" she asked as her mother handed the files to a passing secretary and closed the door.

"First thing this morning we were notified that the firm is in charge of executing the will of Bartholomew Van Morrow, who died last week," replied her mother.

"Executing a will?" Bridget asked.

"Carrying out the provisions of Mr. Van Morrow's will, dear," her mom replied absent-mindedly as she read a message brought into the office by another secretary.

"A will caused all of this commotion?" Bridget asked as she looked outside the door at the mounting chaos.

"Let's go across the street for a snack," Bridget's mom said. "I need to get out of here for a sanity break."

"So, who was this Bartholomew Van Morrow and what's so bad about his will?" Bridget inquired as she and her mother carried bagels and juice to their table.

Her mom explained that Mr. Van Morrow was an eccentric billionaire who spent much of his life exploring the far corners of the world, collecting rare treasures as he went. "During his last years, he had become so obsessed that the younger generation was growing up without a knowledge of geography that he made a special provision in his will—a bequest to give one of his rare treasures, worth $20 million, to the United Nations to sell. The proceeds will go to UNICEF, the United Nations Children's Fund. Imagine how much that could help needy children in the world."

"So what's the problem?" asked Bridget in disbelief.

"It's how the UN is to get the treasure in the first place," her mom replied. "You see, the will says that a team of young people have to use a knowledge of geography to find the treasure by mid-August. If it's not found by the deadline, the UN loses all rights to the treasure."

"Did Mr. Van Morrow name the team who will search for the treasure?" Bridget asked as she finished her juice and popped some fresh bubble gum into her mouth.

"That's the whole problem," sighed her mother as they stood to clear the table. "We've got to get a team together before the end of this week or they'll never have enough time to find the treasure. Every dignitary at the United Nations has been calling us all morning to ask if the firm has a team together yet. You'll have to fix your own dinner tonight, dear, because I'm sure to be working late."

Bridget's mind was racing like a car in the Indy 500, as the way to escape the worst summer of all time took hold. "Mom, I know you've arranged for me to go to that great camp in Maine for the summer," she began, "but I'd be willing to help out with this problem. You know, my friends Babette and Barnaby and I have had some experience in the quest-and-adventure department. We all have the summer off from school, and I could call them this afternoon. Giving up the summer camp would be a disappointment for me, but you know I'd do anything to help you out." She slipped a sideways glance at her mother to see how the sales pitch was being received.

"Well, I don't know..." her mom began.

Seizing the moment, Bridget cried, "Oh, please, Mom! Think of what I'll learn while doing something for a good cause like UNICEF."

Her mother was quiet while they crossed the street and walked back toward the office. Finally she said, "Well, call your friends and see what they and their parents think. I'll call you later this afternoon."

Within half an hour of her mother's phone call, Bridget had contacted Babette and Barnaby. Babette, who finds the tourists who descend on Paris each summer so boring, was willing to get on the next plane out. And Barnaby, whose absent-minded parents had forgotten to register him for the science camp he had planned for the summer, was also eager to go on a new quest. So, they planned to meet at noon three days later at the Statue of Liberty.

"So where are we supposed to start looking for the treasure?" Barnaby asked Bridget as they were waiting for the next ferry to leave Liberty Island.

"All I know is that a sealed envelope is to be delivered to us sometime today," replied Bridget. "I suppose that will give us some clue as to what we're to do first."

Just then, a ferry loaded with tourists arrived, and most were getting off at the island. Bridget, Barnaby, and Babette waited for them to leave the boat before they scurried on deck to find seats.

Beauregard and Luigi were in the ferry lounge, lapping up some berry punch. "Sightseeing in the city can make a cat thirsty," thought Beauregard as he strolled onto the deck. Then, with a small gasp, he noticed Bridget, Barnaby, and Babette sitting on a deck bench, looking out over the harbor. " I should have known!" he thought to himself. He excused himself from Luigi's company to ease closer to the three young people who, he guessed from past experience, were probably in need of his help. He hadn't exactly planned to be spotted but, at his size, it was difficult not to be.

"Beauregard, *mon cheri*!" exclaimed Babette when she saw their old companion. "What are you doing here?"

After explanations all around, it was clear to Beauregard that spending a relaxing summer with Luigi was not to be a reality. "Oh, well," he thought to himself, "such are the responsibilities of a feline of my position and intelligence."

"Where in the world do you think the treasure could be hidden?" asked Bridget to no one in particular as the four old friends sat watching the Statue of Liberty growing smaller in the distance.

"Going on a trip of the world, you say?" said a voice that startled them all. They turned to see a grizzled old man with a faded navy blue jacket, worn trousers, and ragged cap sitting a few feet away on a deck bench.

"Yes, we're going somewhere in the world, I suppose," Bridget responded. "But we don't know where or how far yet."

"You'd better get yourselves familiar with some basics then," exclaimed the old man. "Allow me to introduce myself. I'm Silas Filmore—Yankee-born and world-traveled. I've sailed to every port in the world and explored every continent in my time. There are many things you need to know before traveling the world. For example, you'll need to know about continents, oceans, and longitude and latitude."

"I'm sure we do have a lot to learn, but we've tackled tough adventures before," Bridget stated.

Beauregard overheard Bridget's remark as he was walking away from the group to talk to Luigi, who had taken a seat on the other side of the ferry. "Tackled adventures indeed!" he thought to himself. "Let's not get too big for our boots now. There's been many a tight spot that *I've* had to get you out of!"

Beauregard explained to Luigi that their summer of fun in cool, placid places would have to be postponed indefinitely while he joined Bridget, Barnaby, and Babette on their globetrotting quest for Mr. Van Morrow's treasure. The ferry docked as Beauregard and his friend made plans to rendezvous in Times Square on New Year's Eve.

"If you can spare a few minutes, come with me to my place," said Silas Filmore as the group walked along the dock. "I have a couple of things that could prove quite useful to you in your quest."

The group followed him down a side street and through a narrow alleyway to a studio apartment above a marine supply store.

Silas Filmore rummaged through an old chest in his apartment. Finally, his head reappeared in a small cloud of dust, and in his hand was a large, tattered book titled *The World: An Explorer's Guide*. He gave the book with its well-worn, dog-eared pages to Bridget saying, "This should supply you with lots of information you may need as you make your journey. It includes facts and explanations for just about everything to do with geography. For starters, you'll need to learn about the **hemispheres**, **continents**, and **oceans**. But most important, you must know how to find the specific location of a place by using **longitude** and **latitude**." He continued sharing information from the book as the three kids listened eagerly, and Beauregard catnapped.

"The earth is a large, round object much like a ball or sphere. It rotates around its axis every twenty-four hours. The two ends of the axis are what we call the **poles.** The best way to envision the earth is to use a globe, since it is round like the earth. However, it is difficult to carry globes around everywhere, so we have to use maps in most situations. Maps are flat. In order to present the continents, countries, and other sites as accurately as possible, we must project the round globe onto a flat map. Many systems are used, but none are perfect for all situations and needs. For the most part, you will use the maps in this explorer's guide. **Geographers**, people who study **geography**, which is the physical and cultural characteristics of the earth, divide the earth into spheres. One way to divide the earth is by splitting it into two halves, each of which is called a hemisphere. The left model here shows the earth divided at the **equator**. The half above the equator is called the northern hemisphere and the half below the equator is called the southern hemisphere. Do you follow me, folks?"

"Yes," they all said. This quest looked like it was going to be fun.

"Please continue," Babette urged.

"In the model on the right, the earth is split into two halves from top to bottom, around the North and South Poles. The half on the left is called the western hemisphere and the one on the right is called the eastern hemisphere."

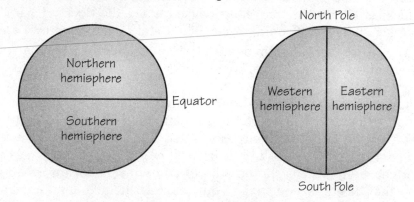

Figure 1: Hemispheres

"Is there anyway that the northern hemisphere and the eastern hemisphere can be placed together?" Bridget interjected.

"Why, yes, Bridget, that's a good question. Actually, it is one of the first ways we begin to locate a specific place. Look at the map here in the book."

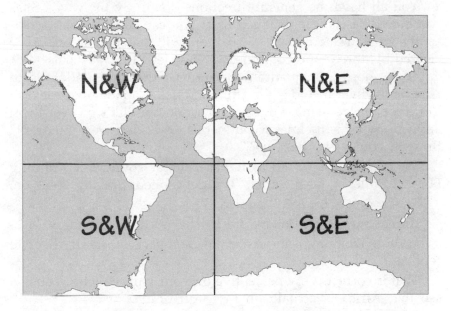

Figure 2: The earth's quadrants

"You can see that if you combine the four different hemispheres and place them on a map or look at them on a globe, there are actually four major areas. In the four parts, you can label the left top as the north and west part, the bottom left as the south and west, the right top as the north and east, and finally the right bottom as the south and east. We call each of these parts a **quadrant**."

"Barnaby," asked the old sailor, "in which quadrant do you live?"

"In the north and west quadrant," answered Barnaby.

"That is correct. You can also call that the northwest quadrant. If you lived in the south and the west, it would be the..."

"Southwest," Bridget shouted, leaping up from her chair. She was getting kind of excited about this trip, but immediately felt a little embarrassed. She sat down again quietly and fidgeted with her hands.

"Absolutely correct," said Silas, pleased with her enthusiasm. "And the north and east would be called what, Babette?"

"That would be the northeast quadrant," Babette replied.

"And, Barnaby, the south and east would be called the..."

"Southeast," exclaimed Barnaby.

"You all have the general directions down. By the way," Silas continued, "as you look at *any* map you can refer to the top left as the northwestern part...well, you will see that later." Silas cleared his throat and continued. "Now, let's look at what we've got in the northwest quadrant. We can see the continent of North America, which includes the United States, Canada, and Mexico. You probably remember these from school, but let's go over them anyway. What is the major continent in the southwest quadrant? Bridget, could you help us?"

"Yes, it's South America. It has several countries, including Bolivia, Chile, and Argentina," Bridget replied, perking up again.

"That's great, Bridget!" smiled Silas.

"Babette, what continents are in the northeast quadrant?"

"It looks like Europe and Asia, and even parts of Africa," Babette replied.

"That is correct. Very perceptive on your part, Babette. You can see that Africa is actually in three quadrants."

Silas then looked at Barnaby and asked, "How about the southeast quadrant?"

"Well, Mr. Filmore, it looks as though the continent of Australia is there, along with several islands. I believe most of the islands are considered part of what is called Oceania."

"And since you brought it up, what is an island?" Silas asked.

"**An island is a body of land that is completely surrounded on all sides by water,**" Barnaby replied, scratching his head. A large chocolate bar fell out of his huge mane of hair. He calmly unwrapped it, broke it into pieces, and shared it with the others.

Silas, somewhat surprised, took the chocolate. "Excellent, my friend, you will learn much more about islands and other land forms as you go on your journey. And it looks like that hair of yours might come in handy, too."

"Who can tell me the name of one more continent?" the old sailor went on.

"The continent of Antarctica, but there is little there except ice," Babette replied.

"That is correct. I hope you don't have to visit Antarctica on your travels. It's mighty cold down that way."

Everybody shivered as if it was cold in the apartment. Beauregard yawned and went back to sleep. "Well, if we do find ourselves there, at least my fur will help to keep me warm," he thought. "But really, we're hardly likely to end up in Antarctica!"

"Just for a review, look at the map and tell me what the four oceans are," Silas was saying.

"That's easy," bragged Barnaby. "The four oceans are the Atlantic, Pacific, Arctic, and Indian. The Pacific Ocean is the largest. In fact, it is slightly larger than the Atlantic and Indian Oceans combined. The Arctic Ocean is the smallest; it covers only about 4 percent of the total oceans." Barnaby pointed to the oceans as he talked. "And," he concluded, "the earth is covered by 70 percent water."

"Wow! I'm very impressed, Barnaby," Silas said. "Where did you learn all that?"

"My mother is quite a keen oceanographer," Barnaby replied. "But physics is more my thing."

Silas looked at the strange kid with bushy hair. Come to think of it, he did look like the scientific type. "Well," he said, "now I want to teach you about **longitude** and **latitude**."

Silas turned a few pages in the old book until he came to a map of the world. "Look at the numbers at the top, bottom, left, and right of this map," he said. (See fig. 3, p. 12.)

"The numbers mark the degrees of longitude and the degrees of latitude. Any point on the earth can be located by using these two tools together. For example, look at the **equator**. It circles the center of the earth. If you took a trip around the equator, you'd travel a distance of 24,902 miles. But, the equator is also known as 0 degrees latitude. We use a little circle to stand for degrees, for example 2° N latitude." He pointed in the book. "Latitude runs east and west but measures north and south. Look at the numbers on the left and right sides of the map. These are degrees of latitude. If you go north it is called north latitude, and if you go south it is south latitude. Look at the line that runs right under most of the United States and near the top of Florida. It is called 30° N latitude. Everyone understand?"

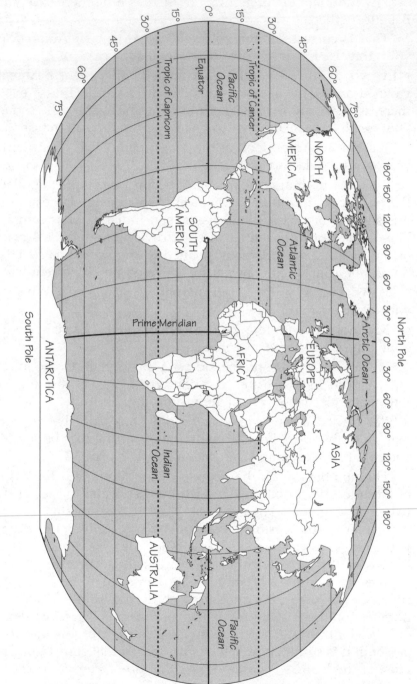

Figure 3: The world

The kids all nodded.

"Good. Now, Barnaby, tell me what you think the lines running north and south or from pole to pole are called," asked the old sailor.

"Those have to be longitude, and I see that 0° longitude is right in the middle of the map. I've heard that the polar circumference around the earth is slightly less than the distance around the equator. Do the numbers at the top and bottom help us figure out how to count longitude?"

"Very observant, Barnaby. That is correct on all counts. Longitude runs from north and south but measures east to west. I know that may sound confusing, but once you get the hang of it, it will be easy," assured Silas. "Yes, Barnaby, the polar circumference in miles around the poles is only 24,860 miles, a little bit shorter than the equatorial circumference. Therefore, the earth is not a perfect sphere, but close enough! Now back to longitude. Degrees of longitude are also called meridians. Look at the 0° longitude at the top of the page. It goes through Greenwich, England and is known as the **prime meridian**. Where does the prime meridian cross the equator, Babette?"

Babette traced the prime meridian down halfway until she came to the equator. "Right here," she said as she pointed to a place that intersected the equator.

"Great, Babette. That point where the two lines intersect or cross each other is called zero degrees longitude and zero degrees latitude. As you can see, it's right off the west coast of Africa at a point in the Atlantic Ocean. That point or place on the earth is also called **absolute location**. It is the exact point where two lines intersect. In fact, we can measure any point on the earth, where the Statue of Liberty stands, or the Empire State Building, or my apartment right where you are standing."

"Totally awesome," Bridget exclaimed. "I bet we'll need to know that as we look for clues."

"Yes, it is different from what we call **relative location**. For example, we can say that the Statue of Liberty, the Empire State Building, and my apartment are all in New York City. However, that doesn't give us the absolute location. That's what's so great about longitude and latitude." The old sailor was obviously wise, and was eager to help the group in their quest for the hidden treasure. "Bridget, go to the point at the top and to the left. Remember the northwest quadrant?"

Bridget nodded that she did.

"Now go along until you find 90° W longitude and go down until the line intersects with the line we used a moment ago, 30° N latitude. Where do the two lines intersect?"

"In the far south of the United States. It looks close to the ocean," Bridget answered.

"That point is called 30 degrees north latitude and 90 degrees west longitude. Yes, it's near the Atlantic Ocean. This ocean in this area is called the Gulf of Mexico. You will learn about gulfs on your travels," Silas assured them.

"What if the point is not on one of the lines?" asked Bridget.

"Excellent question. There are actually 360 lines or degrees of longitude and 180 lines or degrees of latitude. We just don't put all of them on maps, because it would make them too crowded. You have to estimate between the printed numbers. One degree of latitude is 69 miles everywhere on the globe, while one degree of longitude varies from 69 miles at the equator to zero at the pole. Geographers get real specific and divide each degree of longitude and latitude by minutes and seconds. Each degree is divided into 60 minutes and each minute into 60 seconds."

"This is getting a bit heavy, isn't it?" asked Bridget. "We obviously need a magic tool that does all of that for us." The old sailor gave her a sly glance and continued with the lesson.

"Use your estimation skills to see if you can find a point that is 60° N latitude and 85° W longitude. You will have to find the imaginary line that runs halfway between 80 and 90 degrees."

All of the group—except Beauregard, who was still sleeping—worked together to find the assigned point. "It is at a point in Canada in a large lake," Babette answered.

"Correct, but that's no lake. It's a bay. Hudson Bay, to be precise. Now, I think you kids are about ready for your quest. But take this quiz just to double check."

🖐 QUIZ #1 🖐
Quadrants

Use the map below and the world map on page 12 to answer the following questions:

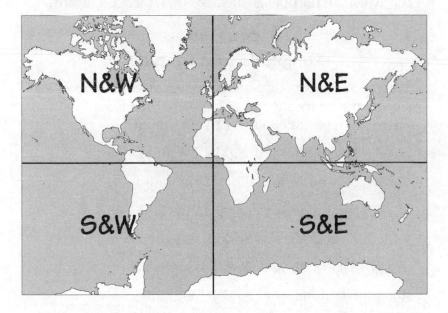

1. Which continent can be found in the northwestern quadrant?

2. Most of the Indian Ocean is located in which quadrant?

3. The majority of South America is located in which quadrant?

4. Antarctica is located in which two quadrants?

5. Which continent is in the NW, NE, and SE quadrants?

6. Most of the Atlantic Ocean is located in which two quadrants?

7. Asia is located in which quadrant?

8. Which ocean is found in the NW and NE quadrants?

9. Which ocean is located in all four quadrants?

10. Most of Europe is located in which quadrant?

✍ QUIZ #2 ✍
Longitude and Latitude

Using the world map on page 12, use the following coordinates to locate and list the continents and oceans where the specific points can be found.

1. 30° N latitude and 60° W longitude

2. 29° S latitude and 120° W longitude

3. 85° S latitude and 68° E longitude

4. 42° N latitude and 135° E longitude

5. 27° S latitude and 138° E longitude

6. 4° N latitude and 76° W longitude

7. 52° N latitude and 46° E longitude

8. 1° S latitude and 16° E longitude

9. 86° N latitude and 2° W longitude

10. 32° S latitude and 62° E longitude

✍ EXERCISE #1 ✍
Using an Atlas

1. Why do degrees of longitude vary in distance and degrees of latitude do not?

2. Using an atlas, list the continents in order of size.

3. Search in the atlas to find the square mileage of the oceans and their greatest depths.

Silas came back into the room and went over the group's responses. "Great job, folks. I'm proud of how quickly you learn. Now, I have something that will help you get to your absolute locations. This is the magic that I was telling you about."

At this, Beauregard decided it was time to wake up. Silas reached into the chest and pulled out an object about the size and shape of a Frisbee. It had buttons and knobs on top, with a small digital readout area in the center. "Looks like some sort of game board," thought Barnaby, as he watched Silas Filmore carefully brush some specks of dust from the surface of the object. Bridget, Barnaby, Babette, and Beauregard gathered closely around as Silas Filmore began to speak.

"This is called a Coordinator," he began. "As far as I know, I'm the only person on earth who has one of these. By dialing the exact longitude and latitude coordinates of a particular location and holding on as this green button is pushed, this machine will transport you to wherever you wish to travel on earth. By using the Coordinator, you should be able to travel more quickly in an effort to make your deadline this summer."

"Wow!" exclaimed Barnaby, eying the machine with a mixture of wonder and respect. "This is like being in a science fiction movie!"

"Oh, I assure you that this machine works through pure science and no fiction," replied Silas Filmore. "But be careful about the coordinates—you'll need to know exactly where you're going!"

"That is yet to be determined," stated Bridget. "We have no idea how this quest is to start, but I suppose we'll find out soon enough."

Silas Filmore rummaged in the large chest once more, and this time reappeared with a well-worn backpack. He put the guidebook and the Coordinator in the pack, presented it to the kids, and wished them well on their travels.

Chapter 2
A Splash in the Great Lakes

After walking several blocks, the four adventurers found themselves back on the busy streets.

"Which way to the subway station?" asked Babette as she looked past the cars whizzing by. Then, out of the corner of her eye, she saw a gleaming black limousine approaching from the left. The limo pulled up to the curb and stopped in front of Bridget, Babette, Barnaby, and Beauregard, who all stepped back for fear the limo would roll over their toes. In silence, the four watched as a uniformed driver with a long, stern-looking face emerged from the vehicle and approached them.

"You are the team designated by the United Nations to find a treasure hidden by the late Bartholomew Van Morrow, I presume?" he asked rather formally, and gave a little sniff.

"Yeah, that's us," said Bridget as she shifted her hands into the pockets of her jeans. She didn't really go for this guy.

"Well, then, this is for you," said the driver as he handed Bridget a metallic cylinder.

"This looks like one of those gizmos you put into the tube system at the bank," thought Bridget as she turned the cylinder around in her hands. "What are we supposed to do with this?" she demanded.

By this time, the driver had already walked back around the car to the door. "That is entirely up to the four of you," he answered. His nose went up in the air, and without another word, he got into the limo and drove off.

"How very formal," Babette commented as she lifted up her sunglasses and squinted in the direction of the disappearing limo. "What do you think this is supposed to mean?"

"I have no idea," replied Bridget. She gave a deep shrug, and something moved inside the cylinder. "Hold it," she said, "it sounds like this has something inside it."

"Let me have it," said Barnaby, looking at the cylinder in a measured, scientific manner. He took the cylinder, turned it around several times, and found a small silver latch at one end. "I think we open it this way," he announced as he pulled the latch. With a shake of the tube, a folded piece of paper emerged and fell to the ground.

The four globetrotters eyed the piece of paper. Finally, Bridget picked it up, unfolded it, and read:

Clue #1 is a gift. The remaining clues will require you to use your knowledge of geography. Good luck! BVM

Clue #1: 42 degrees north latitude and 87 degrees west longitude—You will find warm puppies, cool city cats, windy waves, and smooth sands.

"BVM?" questioned Babette.

"Bartholomew Van Morrow," replied Bridget as she scanned the paper again. "He must have planned all this and written the clues before he died."

"Let's get going then," said Barnaby excitedly, reaching into the backpack and pulling out the Coordinator. "All we need to do is dial in these coordinates and science will do the rest!"

"But don't you think we should check out where 42 degrees north latitude and 87 degrees west longitude is first? And what about these other things like puppies, windy waves, sand, and cool city cats?" questioned Bridget as she pulled Barnaby's itchy fingers away from the Coordinator's knobs.

"We can think about those silly things when we get there," quipped Barnaby as he brushed Bridget's hands away. "This piece of scientific genius will have us all over the world and finding the treasure in no time!"

While Barnaby was turning knobs on the Coordinator, Beauregard was musing over the possible implications of "cool city cats." Suddenly, his daydream was abruptly brought to an end as Babette pulled on his paw saying, "Come on, Beauregard, hold on to the machine! Barnaby has the coordinates set and is ready to push the button!"

Beauregard placed his paws on the machine as the others held on with their hands. "Now let's see what this collection of bells and whistles will do," cried Barnaby as he pushed the green button dramatically.

Splash! Beauregard came up to the top of the water, spluttering and blinking his eyes. He saw Bridget, Babette, and Barnaby pop up nearby. They all started treading water with panicked expressions.

"Where are we?" shouted Babette as she moved closer to the others.

"I don't know," gasped Bridget. "But we've got to do something—quick!"

The four questers looked around for land, but saw nothing but water. Beauregard, being a cat, was particularly upset at finding himself in the middle of a large body of water. He paddled over to Bridget in the hope of using the backpack as a flotation device. In his nervous state, he accidentally pulled the backpack's small outer pocket open with his back paw. As soon as the pocket opened, a pack of Bridget's bubble gum popped up to the surface of the water.

"Hurry, Bridget," urged Babette. "Blow something with your bubble gum to hold us up!"

Bridget grabbed the pack of bubble gum and crammed several pieces into her mouth. She chewed ferociously for a few seconds, then began to blow. The bubble started slowly, but gradually grew and formed itself into the shape of a raft-like boat. A few twists of her lips and quick puffs of air then formed a sail. Bridget tied off the bubble and climbed into the boat, out of breath. Babette and Barnaby followed, pulling Beauregard on board with them.

"The things I get myself into," thought Beauregard indignantly as he sulked in a corner of the boat. "Cats never like water, but for someone of my breeding to be dunked into water like a common alley cat is just over the limit!" He began licking his soaked fur in an effort to regain his dignity.

"Not look up the coordinates before we get there, huh?" snarled Bridget, as she turned to Barnaby.

"Deal with those silly things later. Right, Barnaby?" added Babette with a horrible look on her face.

Barnaby crouched down in the boat, looking sheepishly at his friends. His eyes darted quickly from one face to another while he tried to think of an excuse to justify his lapse of methodological reasoning. He also realized that his normally bushy hair, now soaking wet and plastered to his head, added to his present look of foolishness. He probably looked even worse than Beauregard.

"How was I to know that Bartholomew Van Morrow would give us coordinates that would land us in the middle of some ocean or sea or something?" he replied indignantly.

"*Land* being the operative word. Right, Barnaby?" Bridget said as she reached down into the water and tasted some drops from her fingers. "We're not in an ocean, that's for sure. This is **fresh-water**, not **saltwater**. Let's pull out the guidebook and see if we can find out where we are—that is, if it's not soaked, too," she said, narrowing her eyes at Barnaby.

Babette reached for the backpack and discovered that its inner lining had served as a waterproof barrier, so the guidebook was dry. She pulled the book out and handed it to Bridget. After a few minutes, Bridget located the coordinates. "We seem to be in Lake Michigan, one of the Great Lakes," she informed them.

"Let's see if we can find some information about lakes to help us with this clue," suggested Barnaby as he moved over to take a look at the map in the book.

The book stated:

Lake Michigan is one of the Great Lakes, located in North America. The other Great Lakes are Erie, Superior, Huron, and Ontario. The Great Lakes are freshwater lakes, and the largest is Lake Superior.

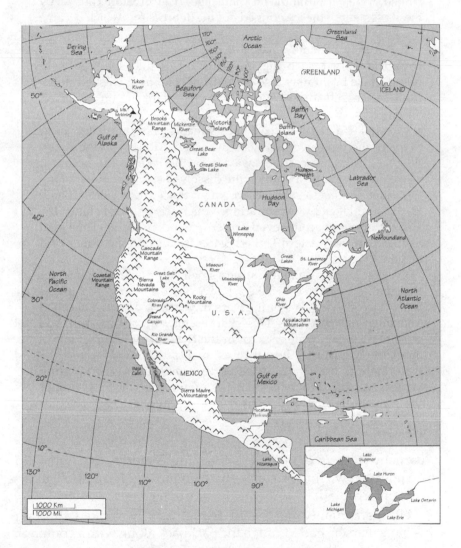

Figure 4: North America

Lakes begin with a depression in the earth's surface. These depressions may occur between hills or mountains or as a result of mudflows or landslides. The depressions that became the Great Lakes were caused by the soil erosion of **glaciers** thousands of years ago.

Glaciers are huge sheets of ice that are in motion. While 5.8 million square miles of the earth are still covered with glaciers, a huge glacier called an **ice shelf** covered Canada and the northern United States thousands of years ago. The erosion caused by the movement of the ice gouged out the depressions which became the Great Lakes.

Lakes may become smaller and disappear over time as the streams filling them bring in sediment, or fine soil. Sediment filling a lake basin may also come from soil being washed down from nearby hillsides or with advancing plant life on the lake's edge.

Most lakes have **outlets** where **streams** take the water away to **rivers** and then, eventually, to the ocean. Along with the water, dissolved salts are carried away from the lake to the ocean. If a lake does not have an outlet, the dissolved salts remain, making the water similar to salty ocean water. Since the water can only leave these lakes by **evaporation**, which leaves salt behind, the lake water may become even saltier than ocean water. The Great Salt Lake in the western United States is an example of this kind of lake.

Creeks, **brooks**, and **streams** are small bodies of running water that may also feed into lakes. However, they may join in the formation of rivers. Water in rivers travels in a depression called a **channel** or **river bed**. This channel may be cut in loose soil or solid rock, and water is kept in the channel by the river banks on each side. During heavy rains, excess water may cause the water in the river channel to rise above the banks, causing **flooding** of nearby land. From its point of origin, a river flows under the influence of **gravity** until it empties into a larger river or an ocean.

"Barnaby, that is extremely interesting material, but what do we do now that we find ourselves in the middle of Lake Michigan?" Babette interrupted.

"Well, it's certainly big," said Barnaby as he looked through some binoculars he had found in the backpack along with a compass.

Bridget held the compass, trying to match the moving arrow with the N representing north. "Land surrounds us, so if we paddle in any direction, we should find the shore and maybe … " Suddenly, gusts of strong winds began to propel the boat westward.

"Quick, Barnaby, look toward the west," shouted Babette after they had been sailing for a while. "I think I can see land!"

Barnaby looked through the binoculars toward the western horizon and exclaimed, "You're right! And it looks like a city—I think I see some tall buildings."

The strong winds continued to sail the boat toward the city, which Bridget had determined by use of the compass and guidebook to be Chicago. They sailed until the lake waves gently guided their boat toward a sandy beach overshadowed by tall buildings. Several early summer beachgoers gawked as they witnessed a bubble gum boat reach shore and deposit three kids and a large black cat onto the sand.

"It looks like we've got wind and sand and a city," said Bridget as she looked at the piece of paper containing Clue #1. "But where are the warm puppies?"

Beauregard, who was still slightly damp, felt a chill as the wind continued to blow. He looked up at the skyscrapers and thought, "I guess this takes care of the 'cool city cats,' too." Being tired and cold also reminded Beauregard that he was hungry. He surveyed the sandy beach for food sources and soon spotted a hot dog stand. Suddenly, his eyes opened wide as he thought of the clue.

"Warm puppies! No, I mean hot dogs!" he exclaimed, pointing out the vendor's stand to Bridget, Barnaby, and Babette. The four questers ran over to the hot dog stand and discovered a metallic cylinder hanging from the counter. The piece of paper in the cylinder contained the following message:

Congratulations on your first success! BVM

Clue #2: 36 degrees north latitude and 112 degrees west longitude—A range carved out from top to bottom.

They all sat on the beach eating hot dogs as Bridget opened the guidebook. "Let's see if we can remember what we have learned about lakes, rivers, and streams," she said.

✍ QUIZ #3 ✍
True or False

State whether the following statements are true or false.

1. Glaciers are huge sheets of ice that are in motion.

2. A large glacier covered the southern United States and Mexico long ago.

3. Lakes begin with a depression in the earth's surface.

4. Soil erosion caused by the movement of a huge glacier called an ice shelf left depressions that later became the Great Lakes.

5. Lakes may become smaller and disappear over time as streams fill them with sediment, or fine soil.

6. Most lakes have outlets whereby streams take the water away to rivers and then to an ocean. These lakes are known as freshwater lakes.

7. If a lake does not have an outlet, the dissolved salts remain. Evaporation is the only way any water can escape. In this case, the lake becomes a saltwater lake.

8. Creeks, brooks, and streams are small bodies of water that run into lakes or help form rivers.

9. Rivers flow under the influence of gravity until they empty into larger rivers or an ocean.

10. The water in a river travels in a depression called a channel. Water is kept in the channel by the river banks on each side.

11. Flooding is caused by evaporation and gravity.

12. The earth is equally divided into 50 percent water and 50 percent land.

✍ EXERCISE #2 ✍
Rivers, Lakes, and Oceans

1. Using the map of North America on page 23, find out what river flows out of Lake Ontario.

2. Using the same map, determine the three rivers that merge into each other in North America to form the major river that flows into the Atlantic Ocean at the Gulf of Mexico.

3. Estimate the order of the Great Lakes according to size.

4. Using the map of South America on page 48, name three or four of the area's major rivers, and determine the oceans into which these rivers flow.

5. Go to the map of Asia on page 93 and locate the Ganges River. Into which ocean does it flow? Look in reference books such as encyclopedias to find out what is so special about the Ganges.

Some Interesting Facts...

- The major lakes in North America are the Great Lakes (Lake Superior, Lake Huron, Lake Erie, Lake Ontario, and Lake Michigan), Lake Winnipeg, Lake Nicaragua, Great Bear Lake, Great Slave Lake, and Great Salt Lake.

- In North America, the major rivers include the Arkansas, Churchill, Colorado, Frazer, Mackenzie, Mississippi, Missouri, Nelson, Ohio, Red, Rio Grande, St. Lawrence, Saskatchewan, Snake, and Yukon.

- The Caspian Sea in Asia is actually a lake. It is the largest natural lake in the world. It covers an area of approximately 143,250 square miles.

- Lake Superior in North America is the second largest lake in the world. It covers an area of approximately 31,800 square miles.

- Lake Manitoba in North America has a maximum depth of only 12 feet.

- Lake Baykal in Asia is the deepest lake in the world, with a maximum depth of 5,316 feet.

- The Nile is the longest river in the world. It runs a length of more than 4,100 miles.

- The Amazon River in South America is the second longest river in the world. It runs a length of almost 4,000 miles.

- The St. Lawrence River and the Rio Grande in North America are similar in length, at approximately 1,900 miles.

- The Colorado River in North America is approximately 900 miles long.

✎ ✎ ✎ ✎ ✎

"We're going to check out these coordinates before Barnaby gets his hot little hands on the Coordinator this time," said Bridget as she turned the pages. "Let's see…it looks like we're going to the southwestern United States, near the Grand Canyon."

"That sounds much safer than landing in the middle of Lake Michigan," replied Babette as she wiped a spot of mustard from her mouth. "Shall we trust Barnaby with the Coordinator again?"

Beauregard glanced at the guidebook to recheck the accuracy of the location as Barnaby began setting the Coordinator.

"Okay, everyone," said Barnaby, "hold on to the Coordinator. We're ready to travel!"

A quick push of the green button sent the globetrotters into a rapid spin that ended when their feet touched a dry, dusty trail.

Bridget, Barnaby, Babette, and Beauregard looked around, recognizing a landscape they'd seen from pictures of the Southwest. They walked along the trail a few minutes and came to a spot where the ground just seemed to stop. Looking down, they saw a huge hole in the earth, with dips and rises in its walls, that descended to a river at the bottom. From this height, the river looked like a narrow blue ribbon.

"Sure is a long way down, isn't it?" a voice behind them said. Jumping slightly with surprise, the questers turned to see a person in old brown, baggy trousers, plaid shirt, brown vest, and a dingy felt hat that had lost its shape long ago. A closer look revealed that the person was a woman about sixty years old. With one hand she held on to a mule, with the other she rubbed her eyes. "Dust everywhere," she said. "But you'll get used to it."

"You startled us," said Bridget. "Is that the Grand Canyon we just about fell into?"

"Sure is!" replied the woman cheerfully. "I didn't mean to scare you, but if you don't mind me remarking, you folks don't exactly look like you belong here. That cat, for instance, is going to find it mighty hot down this way."

Beauregard gave a low, anguished sort of growl. Yes, he knew it was hot. Why hadn't he just settled for the verandah?

"My name is Polly," the woman was saying. "Prospector Polly is what most folks around here call me. I've spent most of my days here around the canyon and know just about every inch by now. Why, I could go down there blindfolded. So, what brings you here?"

"We're on a kind of treasure hunt, I guess you could say," Barnaby answered, looking a little troubled. "We're going from place to place based on clues. Here's the one that brought us here."

Prospector Polly read the clue and said, "That top to bottom part probably means you'll need to travel down to the bottom of the canyon. Have any of you ever done that sort of traveling?" Polly was being polite. It was pretty obvious the questers were city slickers who had probably never even seen a mule, let alone ridden one.

"Well, not exactly," Bridget began as she looked around at the others. "Is there a road or anything we can take to get there?"

"A road?" Polly laughed. "The best you'll do is a trail a few feet wide!" Then, noting the disheartened looks on the faces of the questers, she added, "But if you want, I'll round up four more mules and take you down there myself."

"Oh, yes…please," Babette replied. "We would be very grateful."

"Come on then," motioned Polly. "It'll take long enough as it is without us wasting time talking about it. If we don't hurry up, we'll be going down there in pitch darkness!"

The questers gingerly followed Polly to her cabin, where they loaded supply packs and strapped them to the mules standing patiently outside. Then they all climbed onto the mules and set off down a narrow trail on the side of the canyon, with Polly leading the way. Occasionally, a stone would break away from the side of the trail and fall far down into the canyon. "Paris, even with the tourists, would not have been this miserable," thought Babette as she wiped the dust from her face.

Figure 5: A canyon

Bridget, however, was not so bothered by the dust and heat. "This scenery is spectacular, Polly," she remarked, looking around at the canyon. "I can see why you have stayed here so long."

"This is a fascinating place, all right," replied Polly. "Let me tell you something about it while we ride down the trail."

Polly began her lesson, "As you may know, mountains are the highest points on the continents and are also where many rivers of the world originate. The direction in which a river flows is determined by the mountains, and this is called the **continental divide**. There may be one or more continental dividing points for rivers on a continent, but either way it is determined by the highest mountain point of the region. For example, there is a continental divide in the United States running through the Rocky Mountains.

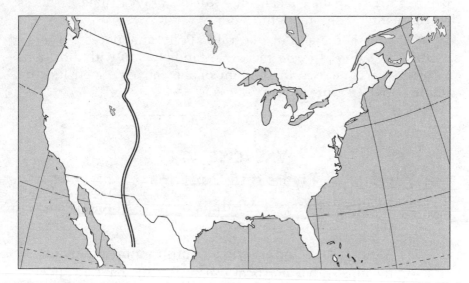

Figure 6: Western U.S. Continental Divide

All the rivers east of this divide flow into the Atlantic Ocean, while those west of the divide flow into the Pacific Ocean. And what's all this got to do with canyons? Well, the rapid flow of water from a stream or river can cause a depression in the earth called a gully, ravine, gorge, or canyon, depending on the size. These depressions have deep, steep walls caused by the erosion of the rock by the water currents over time. And you're looking at a beaut! The Colorado River carved out the Grand Canyon over millions of years, leaving a depression that is 217 miles wide and more than a mile deep."

Polly took a deep breath. Feeling pleased with the information she had given the travelers, she was now content to remain quiet for the rest of the journey. It was time for them all to take in the greatness of the Grand Canyon.

Many hours later, the weary group of adventurers reached the bottom of the canyon. Beauregard was stretched out sideways over the saddle, looking like a furry pack on the mule. "How will I ever be able to slink across a room with my graceful feline glide again?" he groaned. "Every inch of my body has been bounced and pummeled by this mule. And just look at my fur!"

Babette looked equally distressed. Her black ensemble, like Beauregard's fur, had taken on a dusty, grayish tone. "This is so disgusting," she thought, wiping her brow.

"Well, this is the end of the trail," Polly announced. "There's a ranger's station just over there. He can help you with directions to other places here at the bottom of the canyon. Good luck on finding that treasure of yours."

✍ EXERCISE #3 ✍
Rivers and Canyons

1. Look at the map of Australia on page 81 and locate the continental divide.

2. Melting snow forms swift streams in some mountain terrains. What practical use could this have for us?

3. Look at several maps that show the continents. Use your critical thinking ability to determine why rivers are so important on continents.

4. Use your library skills to research and write a report on how rivers can carve great ravines and canyons into the land. Present your report to others.

5. Take notes the next time it rains heavily in your area. Check places that have limited grass coverage and describe how a gully is formed. Take pictures and use this for a project later in school.

≪ ≪ ≪ ≪ ≪

The group thanked Polly for her help and waved good-bye as she disappeared around a curve in the trail. Bridget, Barnaby, and Babette picked up their supplies and walked in the direction of the ranger's station, as Beauregard trailed wearily behind.

"Welcome to the Grand Canyon," said the ranger as the questers entered the station. "You look like you could use a rest. Come on in and sit down."

The three kids stretched out on the comfortable chairs provided by the ranger. Beauregard declined a seat, instead lying flat out on the floor in a most uncharacteristic manner.

"We're not used to trails and mule rides," Bridget explained, leaning down to pet Beauregard's head. "We've come here from New York City."

"New York City!" exclaimed the ranger. "You aren't by any chance the group on some sort of mission for the United Nations, are you?"

"Why, yes, we are," Barnaby replied, perking up with interest. "We are on a treasure hunt to help UNICEF."

"Then I have a package for you. It arrived a few days ago," stated the ranger as he pulled out a brown paper package addressed to: "United Nations UNICEF Team, c/o Ranger's Station, Grand Canyon."

"Range...Ranger Station!" exclaimed Babette as she thought of the clue.

Bridget opened the package to find a metallic cylinder with another message inside:

Dusty and sore from the ride? Congratulations on your fortitude! BVM

Clue #3: 18 degrees north latitude and 78 degrees west longitude—Cruises and calypso, snorkeling and coral reefs.

"Mmmm...cruises and calypso," thought Babette. "That sounds much better than dust and mules to me!"

"It looks like the coordinates are very close to water, Bridget," stated Barnaby as he looked in the guidebook. "You'd better get the bubble gum ready just in case we need it."

They helped Beauregard up from the floor, and said thank you and good-bye to the ranger.

"I'm sorry we can't stay longer," Bridget added apologetically. "But as you can see, our furry friend here has a particular problem with the heat."

Barnaby set the knobs on the Coordinator, and the four questers grabbed hold of it.

"Caribbean, here we come!" shouted Barnaby as he pressed the green button.

The ranger looked astonished. In a flash, all that was left of his visitors were three smallish depressions in his chairs and a large, dusty outline of a cat on his floor. "Maybe this heat is getting to me too, these days," he wondered.

Chapter 3
Off to the Caribbean!

When the four adventurers focused their eyes again, they were looking past palm trees and a sandy white beach toward a Caribbean sunset that seemed to contain every color of the rainbow.

"Do you hear that?" exclaimed Babette. "Calypso music! Oh, it makes me want to dance!"

"Looks like you're not the only one, Babette," Bridget replied, pointing down the path.

Beauregard, it seemed, had gotten over his last ordeal fairly quickly. The large black cat swayed his tail and moved his paws to the beat as he walked on ahead of them.

"He seems lost in the beat," Bridget concluded.

Actually, Beauregard was lost in the memory of another Caribbean adventure as he moved down the path toward the music and the beach. "Juanita, my little calypso kitten," he smiled dreamily. "We danced together so many nights on the beach. My quest for pirate's treasure took me away that summer...ah, but the memories."

"Hey, it looks like there's going to be a party on the beach!" Barnaby exclaimed, jolting Beauregard out of his pleasant reminiscence.

As the four friends continued down the path, they could see people setting up food tents on the beach and lighting tall torches stuck into the sand. The catchy, rhythmic songs of the calypso band grew louder as they approached.

"There's a sign over there where everyone is going into the party," said Bridget. "Let's go over and see what it says."

The four approached the large sign beside the two torches that marked the entrance to the party. It read:

Paradise Cruise Lines welcomes you to Montego Bay!
We hope you enjoy the beach party and will
take part in one of tomorrow's activities while
we are in port:
8 a.m.—Exploring island treasures
9 a.m.—Shopping in town
10 a.m.—Coral reef snorkeling
All groups will leave from the Lido Deck of the
ship. Have a great time!

"Montego Bay…" said Barnaby thoughtfully as he scratched his head. At that, a brightly colored floral shirt and a garland of tropical flowers fell from his hair onto the sand at his feet. "Maybe we should look at our guidebook for more information," he concluded, calmly picking up the shirt and the garland.

Even Babette, Bridget, and Beauregard, who were used to seeing all kinds of things emerge from Barnaby's huge mane of hair, were amazed that it could contain objects that big.

"I wondered where this went," Barnaby continued as he held up the shirt. "It went missing in a rain forest in Australia when I was studying the unique environment of the area," he added, putting the floral shirt on over his lab coat and placing the flowers around Beauregard's neck. "Well, let's get this information together and get on with the party," he exclaimed excitedly as he pulled the guidebook out of the backpack.

The four questers sat down on the sand near the torches to read. Barnaby thumbed through the book for a few minutes until he located the information they needed. Then he began to share the contents with his friends:

"Montego Bay is located on the northwest coast of the island of Jamaica. An **island** is land surrounded by water on all sides. Islands may be found all over the world in every ocean and may be quite large or very small. Greenland is the world's largest island.

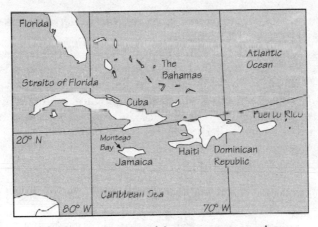

Figure 7: The Caribbean—West Indies

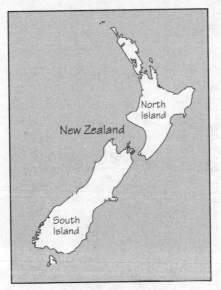

Figure 8: Islands

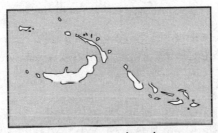

Figure 9: Archipelago

A group of islands or an area of water that contains many islands is called an **archipelago**.

Islands may be located in a bay or gulf near large land masses. A **bay** is a body of water that penetrates a coastline and is often widest at its center. A bay may serve as a site for seaports. **Gulfs** partially enclose a circular coastline and are larger than bays. Jamaica is in the Gulf of Mexico, which is bordered by the coastlines of the United States and Mexico."

Figure 10: Bay

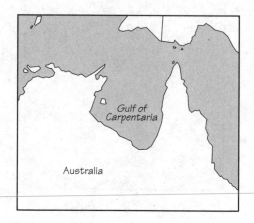

Figure 11: Gulf

"Do bays have to be a particular size?" asked Babette as she looked at the map containing Jamaica and Montego Bay.

"No," replied Barnaby. "They may be as small as Montego Bay or as large as the Bay of Bengal, along the southern coast of Asia."

Looking over Babette's shoulder at the map, Bridget stated, "There are quite a few islands in this area. What makes an island anyway?"

After turning a few pages in the guidebook, Barnaby replied:

"Islands may be formed by a collection of coral, the skeletons of small sea creatures called polyps. As the coral accumulates, reefs are formed under the water's surface. **Coral reefs** provide underwater shelter for many species of fish and other residents of the sea. If enough coral accumulates, it pushes above the water's surface to form an island. Islands may also be created by volcanic action or mountain formation that pushes land up from the ocean floor.

A circular coral island can form on top of a submerged **volcano**, forming an **atoll**. A **lagoon** may occur when a circular island forms and separates a small body of water from the rest of the ocean. These lagoons may be quite deep."

Figure 12: Atoll and lagoon

"The islands in this part of the Atlantic Ocean were the ones the early explorers like Columbus sailed to on their voyages of discovery," Bridget remarked, remembering her history classes at school.

"Why did they choose this area?" Babette asked.

"Because the weather was so nice," thought Beauregard as he stretched out on the sand and let the soft, warm winds float over him.

"I think it was because the **trade winds** and **ocean currents** brought them this way," Bridget responded. "Barnaby, does the guidebook say anything about trade winds and currents?"

"I think I saw something about that over here," Barnaby said as he thumbed back a few pages. He found the information and began to read again:

"Ocean currents may be thought of as 'underwater rivers' that direct water from one part of the ocean to another. Wind, water

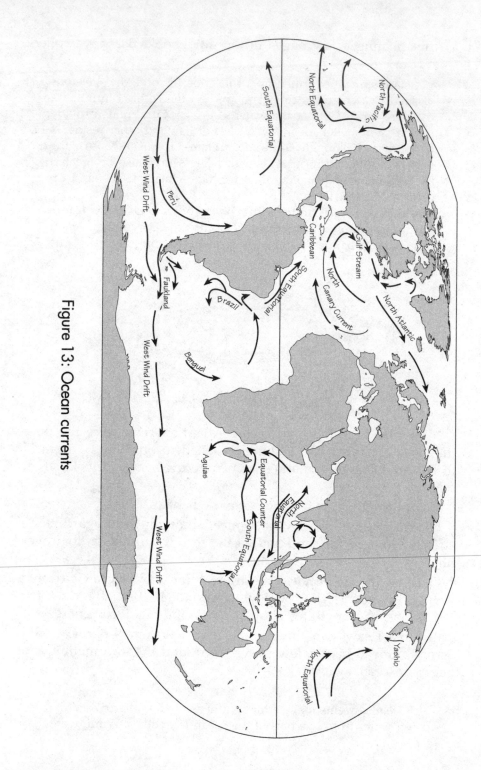

Figure 13: Ocean currents

temperature, and the earth's rotation are major forces directing the path of ocean currents.

"Warm air around the equator rises until it descends at around 30 to 40 degrees north or south latitude. Its descent causes trade winds that blow back toward the equator and westerlies that blow toward the polar regions. Because of the earth's rotation, these winds tend to blow diagonally instead of directly north or south. The warm air and low pressure areas of the equator and tropical ocean regions can give rise to violent ocean windstorms, called **hurricanes** in the Atlantic Ocean, **typhoons** in the Pacific Ocean, and **cyclones** in the Indian Ocean.

"The warm water of the equator travels toward the **poles**, like the equatorial winds. Because water from the equator flows toward either pole, there is little mixing of water from the northern and southern hemispheres. As the warm water travels along this path, the cold water near the poles sinks to the ocean depths. The cold polar water moves along the ocean floor toward the equator, where the water is less dense. Besides its effect on ocean currents, this cooler water may rise up near the shores of continents to help support large fish populations.

"The rotation of the earth causes the Coriolis force. The Coriolis force causes currents to travel clockwise (to the right) in the northern hemisphere, and counterclockwise (to the left) in the southern hemisphere. A quick glance at a map showing ocean currents formed in the North Atlantic will illustrate a clockwise flow, while those in the South Atlantic will show a counterclockwise flow.

"The Gulf Stream is a famous ocean current. It has its origins in the trade winds blowing in a southwesterly direction in the North Atlantic Ocean. Warm water rising from the equator is propelled by the trade winds until it intersects land along the western boundary of the Atlantic, causing the current to deflect northward. The Gulf Stream current, which is about 50 miles wide and moves at 5 miles an hour, was drawn on a map by Benjamin Franklin over two hundred years ago. He suggested that, in order to speed mail from Great Britain to the American colonies, westward-bound ships should avoid the easterly flowing Gulf Stream. As the Gulf Stream flows toward Greenland, arctic currents and the Coriolis force deflect it toward northern Europe. The warm water of the Gulf Stream causes the temperatures of Ireland, Great Britain, and other parts of western Europe to be on average 20 degrees Fahrenheit warmer than other areas of the world with the same latitude. After reaching Europe, the current of the Gulf Stream turns westward as it becomes part of the Equatorial Current.

"The West Wind Drift current encircles Antarctica. This current is also responsible for carrying cool air and water to the south-western coasts of Africa, Australia, and South America."

"Sailors have to learn a lot to navigate the oceans," observed Babette, "just like we do if we are to find the treasure for UNICEF."

✍ EXERCISE #4 ✍
Review

1. Tell your parents or friends at least two ways that islands are formed.

2. Are there differences between an island and an archipelago? If so, what is the major difference?

3. How are a gulf and a bay similar?

4. Impress your teacher by describing the process by which coral forms an island. Make a series of drawings to illustrate the process.

5. From the world of television, figure out why there is a lagoon near Gilligan's Island.

6. How was Columbus's route influenced by the ocean currents and trade winds?

7. What are three things that direct underwater rivers or ocean currents?

8. What does the Coriolis force do? How does it differ in the northern and southern hemispheres?

9. Why are there no hurricanes off the Pacific Ocean and no typhoons off the Atlantic?

10. How do the ocean currents affect the weather of lands far away from their original sources?

"**N**ow that we know more about where we are, let's check out that clue again," said Bridget, pulling the piece of paper from the backpack.

"We already have the cruise ship in port," said Babette, "and we can hear the calypso music. That leaves the coral reef and snorkeling. Perhaps we need to join that group at 10 o'clock tomorrow morning."

"But that's for the cruise passengers," Bridget replied.

"So let's act like passengers!" said Beauregard over his shoulder as he entered the party with dainty, dance-like steps, the garland of flowers swaying gently around his neck.

"Beauregard seems very at home here, doesn't he?" Barnaby commented as the three kids stood up to follow their fascinating feline friend.

Bridget, Babette, and Barnaby joined the party on the beach with Beauregard and the cruise passengers. They sampled dishes of fresh fruit and spicy rice, and drank delicious tropical fruit juices. Then, sometime after midnight, they decided it was time to mingle among a group of passengers who had mentioned going back to the ship soon.

"Just blend in like this," said Bridget, strolling around behind the passengers. "And no one will realize we're not supposed to be on board tonight."

"Where is Beauregard?" Babette asked suddenly, as the passengers were preparing to leave.

"Over there," sighed Barnaby, as he spied Beauregard among a group of party goers in the middle of a limbo contest.

Being so agile, cats can easily bend backward and walk under the outstretched limbo stick in rhythm to the music. Moreover, it wasn't as though Beauregard hadn't performed the limbo before. He remembered very well how he used to impress his dates. "But here comes Bridget," he thought as he spied his young friend out the corner of his eye, though he kept his head pointing forward.

"Come on, Beauregard!" Bridget hissed as she pulled him out of the line of remaining limbo contestants.

"That contest was mine!" sniffed Beauregard indignantly as he moved toward the ship with Bridget, Barnaby, Babette, and the group of passengers. "The sacrifices I have to make in order to look after you three!"

Without cabins to go to, the four explorers decided to hide under an empty lifeboat for the night, which wasn't as uncomfortable as you might imagine, since Beauregard acted as a large, furry pillow, even though he was still miffed about the limbo contest.

The next morning, however, the pillow was already scouting the deck when the others awakened and peered out from beneath the lifeboat tarp.

"I'm going to leave the snorkeling to you three this morning," Beauregard called from the side of the pool. "I've found a deck chair in the perfect spot for relaxing while you're gone."

"I guess you won't be swimming in that pool, either?" Bridget raised her eyebrows as she, Barnaby, and Babette walked toward the Lido Deck to rendezvous with the snorkeling group.

Beauregard pretended not to hear as he nestled into the deck chair for a peaceful morning. "Cats are not *meant* to get wet," he grumbled to himself. "Everybody knows that!"

The snorkeling group boarded a smaller boat, which took them toward a coral reef at the edge of the bay. The leader went over some last minute instructions, then the snorkeling began.

"I can hardly believe how beautiful the tropical fish are on this reef!" exclaimed Babette when the friends came up for a rest.

"Remember to keep your eyes open for a clue cylinder, too," reminded Bridget as they prepared to dive back under the clear blue water.

A moment later, Barnaby was observing a particularly interesting school of small, bright yellow fish when his eyes caught the gleam of an object reflecting a ray of sunshine that beamed through the water.

"A cylinder!" he thought excitedly as he swam toward the metallic tube anchored to part of the reef by a sturdy rope. Barnaby caught his friends' attention and the three of them were soon removing the cylinder from its anchor. They took it back to the cruise ship and ran excitedly over to Beauregard's deck chair.

"We found the cylinder!" they shouted as they neared Beauregard, who slightly lifted one eyelid to see what all the excitement was about. After glimpsing the cylinder, however, Beauregard soon became fully alert, and joined his friends in reading the next clue:

May the trade winds speed you on your journey! BVM

Clue #4:   2 degrees south latitude and 56 degrees west longitude—Look for rains to replace the trade winds, but the tropics remain. For rope, food, or other supplies, travel east to Pedro's Place!

"So, let's get going," said Bridget as she pulled the Coordinator out of the backpack. "I'm going to set the knobs this time, Barnaby."

"Is everybody ready?" Bridget asked after she set the latitude and longitude coordinates for their next destination. Babette and Beauregard turned longingly toward the palm trees on the shore and sighed as a tranquil breeze floated across the deck. Slowly, they reached out to hold on to the Coordinator...

_____

Chapter 4
South America and Rain Forests

When their heads stopped whirling from the latest Coordinator trip, the four questers became aware of the sounds of what seemed like thousands of birds and insects. They were standing in a small clearing surrounded by thick vegetation. Babette looked up to see a roof of leaves and trees that allowed only a hint of sunlight to peek through. "Where are we?" she asked Bridget, who was still holding the Coordinator.

"We're only 2 degrees south latitude, so we're near the equator," replied Bridget, beginning to blush as she realized she'd forgotten to check their destination before using the Coordinator. "I gave Barnaby such a rough time about landing in Lake Michigan, and now I did it myself," she thought to herself.

Since no one else seemed to realize her error in judgment, Bridget went on, "This looks like a picture of a rain forest that I saw in a magazine recently. But, just to be sure, let's check out our coordinates and see what the guidebook says."

Bridget pulled the guidebook out of the backpack after carefully storing the Coordinator. After flipping through a few maps she announced, "We're in the middle of a huge **rain forest** near the Amazon River in South America.

"Oh, this is great," thought Beauregard as he swatted an unidentified insect away with his paw. "I get caught up in an adventure that takes me to places that are hotter and more humid than South Carolina. Surely with all these trees there must be a cooler, shady spot around here somewhere."

Figure 14: South America

Beauregard strolled away from the group as Barnaby said, "When I was in Australia studying rain forests, I came to see just how important they are to our environment. In fact, I did a major presentation to an environmental group."

Bridget and Babette could see the scientific spark light up in Barnaby's eyes. "There will be no stopping him now," Bridget whispered to Babette, "so we might as well listen and maybe learn something that will help us get out of here."

"Rain forests grow in layers," Barnaby began, "with the tallest trees sometimes growing to over 200 feet. Beneath them are shorter trees and thick vegetation, which are home to a great variety of animals, birds, and insects."

Babette brushed a mosquito off her arm as Barnaby continued, "In fact, almost two-thirds of all the species of plants and animals on earth are found in rain forests, and many haven't even been cataloged or studied yet. We may find uses for some of these plants we don't yet know about—they may have special medicinal properties, for example!"

Excited about the scientific possibilities, Barnaby began to pace and wave his arms about as he talked. "Rain forests are also renewable resources that are important for people all over the world. The vegetation serves as the earth's 'lungs,' since plants take in carbon dioxide in the air and give off oxygen. An acre of trees can take in 10 tons of carbon dioxide in a year! When you think about our world population and pollution, it becomes clear why rain forests are so important to the earth's **ecology**."

"I saw some university students in Paris protesting about the destruction of rain forests last year," commented Babette. "So the destruction of the rain forests would hurt our environment and make pollution worse?"

"Exactly!" Barnaby cried, his hair springing to new heights. "Tropical rain forests now cover about 6 percent of the earth's surface, but about 50 million acres of rain forest are being destroyed every year. This decreases the amount of carbon dioxide that can be taken in and oxygen that can be given off. In addition, brush is often burned when rain forests are destroyed, and this adds to the pollution in the atmosphere. The total effect of the destruction and pollution is global warming, which creates weather changes and possible flooding from melting polar ice."

"So why not just replant the forest area?" asked Babette.

"It's not that simple!" stated Barnaby, pacing hard across the clearing. "Rain forests can't grow back once they've been cut down. The soil is very poor in nutrients and deteriorates even more after a few years. If the forest is cut down to clear land for farms, crops won't even grow after a few years and the land is often abandoned."

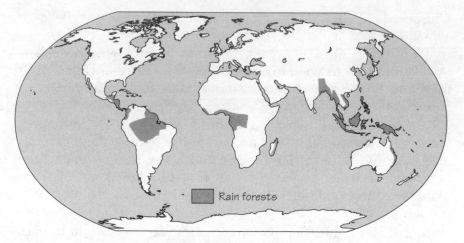

Figure 15: Rain forests of the world

"Well, things seem to grow quite well here now," observed Bridget as she looked around at the thick vines nearby.

"That's because the decaying leaves from the vegetation nourishes the plant life," Barnaby explained. "Without the trees and leaves, the nourishment is gone. And when the crops fail to grow, these areas eventually become wasteland."

"Why do people continue to destroy the rain forests if they know the soil is so poor?" asked Babette, thinking of the protesters in Paris.

"Some people may not know that before they clear the land," Barnaby replied. "But there are other reasons why rain forests are being destroyed, too—growing populations that need places to live, industries that need raw materials, ranches that need grazing land for cattle, forestry and building needs, and mineral exploration. The ways the land and people influence each other get very complex."

"That's a topic for lots of discussion later," interrupted Bridget. "Right now, we've got to get moving if we're going to get out of here and find the next clue. We have a time limit, remember?"

By this time, Beauregard was walking back toward the kids, having failed to find even one cool spot. He suggested that they travel toward the huge river he had discovered beyond a particularly thick stand of vegetation. "We're certainly not going to find anything standing here," he said glumly, "except heat and insects."

✍ QUIZ #4 ✍
Checking Out Rain Forests

Barnaby presented some excellent information about rain forests to the environmental group. He made the presentation again to his three friends when they landed in the rain forest. Help the questers recall the basic facts.

Copy the following sentences into your workbook, filling in the blanks.

1. Rain forests grow in layers, with the tallest trees sometimes reaching over _____ feet in height.

2. Beneath the tallest trees in a rain forest are shorter trees and thick vegetation, which are home to a great variety of _____, _____, and _____.

3. Almost _____ of all the species of plants and animals on earth are found in rain forests, and many haven't been cataloged or studied yet.

4. Some of the plants that we don't know about yet might even have _____ _____ _____!

5. Rain forests are also renewable resources that are important for people all over the world. All of the vegetation serves as the _____ _____, since plants take in carbon dioxide in the air and give off _____.

6. An acre of trees can take in _____ tons of carbon dioxide in a year! When you think about our world population and pollution, it becomes clear why rain forests are so important to the earth's ecology.

7. Tropical rain forests now cover about _____ percent of the earth's surface, but about _____ million acres of rain forest are being destroyed every year.

8. When rain forests are destroyed, this _____ the amount of carbon dioxide that can be taken in and oxygen that can be given off.

9. Brush is often burned when rain forests are destroyed, and this adds to _____ in the atmosphere.

10. The total effect of the destruction and pollution is _____ _____, which creates weather changes and possible flooding from melting _____ ice.

11. Rain forests can't grow back once they have been cut down. The soil is very poor in _____ and deteriorates even more after a few years.

12. If a rain forest has been cut down to clear the land for farms, even _____ won't grow after a few years.

13. _____ _____ from the vegetation nourishes the plant life. Without the trees and leaves, the nourishment is gone.

14. Once crops fail to grow, the area often eventually becomes _____.

15. There are other reasons why rain forests are being destroyed. These include growing _____ that need places to live, industries that need _____ _____, ranches that need grazing land for cattle, forestry and building needs, and _____ exploration.

✍ QUIZ #5 ✍
Search and Find

1. Using the map of the world on page 12, list all the continents in which there are rain forests.

2. In which two continents do most of the rain forests appear?

3. In which part of South America can you find the largest areas of rain forest?

The four friends reached the banks of the river Beauregard had described. "I presume this is the Amazon," Babette said.

"I guess so," replied Bridget cautiously. "But let me see what the guidebook says first."

Bridget found South America and the Amazon River in the guidebook and read the passage to the others:

> "The Amazon River, the largest river in the world, begins in the Andes Mountains of western South America and flows east to the Atlantic Ocean. Smaller rivers, called tributaries, feed into the Amazon along its 400-mile length. The river is so large at its end that fresh water can be detected 50 miles into the Atlantic Ocean. The river and its tributaries form the Amazon River Basin, which drains approximately 35 percent of South America's area."

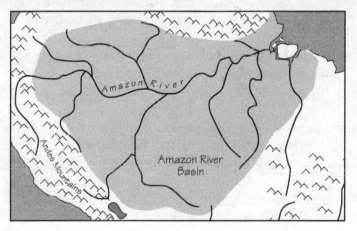

Figure 16: The Amazon River Basin

"Wow! Look at the size of that **river basin**!" exclaimed Barnaby as he looked at the map in the guidebook. "I wonder how the size of the basin was determined?"

"It looks like they found the beginnings of the river and all its tributaries and connected those points to form the shape and size of the basin," replied Bridget after studying the map for a few minutes. "It looks like some of the tributaries are as big as many rivers in the world."

"Then we do not know if we are on the banks of the Amazon River itself or a tributary," said Babette.

"That's right," Bridget replied. "But the clue said to 'travel east to Pedro's Place,' so that means we have to go downriver, since all the water will eventually flow toward the east coast of South America."

"Travel is the key word here," thought Beauregard as he surveyed the wide, rapidly flowing river. "I have no desire to go backstroking down the Amazon."

Suddenly, Beauregard saw some nearby plants move. He motioned to the others to be quiet. The questers moved quietly forward and peered through the thick vines. Four boys, who looked like native people of the area, were pulling a raft toward the water's edge.

Bridget scrutinized the boys. "We sure could use their raft," she whispered. "I'm not sure how long a bubble boat would hold up in that river."

"Maybe they'll trade something for it," suggested Beauregard, envisioning the raft as the safest, driest form of travel available to them right now.

The four friends searched among their possessions for something to trade, but nothing really seemed appropriate. Barnaby began to scratch his head, saying, "There has to be something they would want..."

Bridget, Babette, and Beauregard watched with astonishment as Barnaby stopped in mid-scratch and pulled out a boom box.

"So that's where I put it the other week!" exclaimed Barnaby as he held up the boom box. "I was playing a particularly good CD, as I recall." He pushed the "play" button, forgetting all about hiding from the native boys with the raft, and Mozart's Fourth Symphony filled the forest.

Obviously, the boys were startled by the sudden music. They looked all around, perplexed. Not seeing any imminent danger, however, they seemed to relax and even begin to enjoy the music.

"That's it!" said Bridget in hushed excitement. "We'll offer to exchange the boom box and CD for their raft!"

Cautiously, the four questers came from behind the vines and approached the native boys, who began pointing at the boom box and talking rapidly in a language unknown to the questers—except Babette, that is. Babette, much to the amazement of the others, began speaking with the boys in what sounded like Portuguese, pointing at the boom box then at the raft as she did so. In a few minutes, the trade was a done deal. Babette shook hands with the boys, handed over the boom box, and the boys and Mozart's Fourth disappeared into the forest.

"So, how do we get this thing going?" asked Bridget, surveying their new mode of river transportation.

"You three push it off the bank while I make sure it stays on course," replied Beauregard, who had already hopped onto the raft.

"Don't want to get wet, huh?" said Bridget as she, Babette, and Barnaby pushed the raft into the river and jumped quickly aboard.

Beauregard ignored the comment. "Cats are not *meant* to get wet," he grumbled to himself.

The questers maneuvered the raft into the center of the river to avoid snagging on sandbanks or bends near the edge. It moved slowly along and, as they stretched out, the sounds of the rain forest and the water lulled them into an easy slumber.

A dream of fresh croissants from her favorite Parisian bakery reminded Babette of her hunger as she slowly awakened from her nap. She reached for the backpack to search for something to eat, but found nothing. "We need to get some supplies for this trip," she thought to herself.

Just then, Babette looked toward the left river bank and saw a row of shacks at the water's edge. The shacks were supported above the water by large poles or stilts with ladders. Suddenly, she became aware of a sign on one of the structures—"Pedro's Place: Supplies."

"Wake up, everybody!" Babette yelled. "Here's Pedro's Place, the place the clue talked about!"

Bridget, Barnaby, and Beauregard quickly roused to attention and looked in the direction of Babette's gesturing. Within seconds, they were all paddling fiercely. Soon enough, the raft was next to the ladder leading up to Pedro's.

"We need to get some food," said Babette. "I'm starving."

"Me too," said Barnaby. "But some of us will need to stay on the raft to hold it still. Why don't you climb up, Babette, and go get the food."

"And get me some bubble gum! Oh, yeah, look for a cylinder,

too," Bridget added. "The clue mentioned this place, so maybe the next one will be in there."

Bridget, Barnaby, and Beauregard held the raft steady as Babette climbed the ladder to Pedro's Place. After several minutes, she emerged carrying a burlap sack closed with a drawstring.

"Lunchtime," Babette announced as she released the ladder after feeling both feet safely back on the raft. "I got plenty of food for now and later."

"But what about a cylinder?" asked Bridget.

"Didn't see one," replied Babette, "and I looked all over that store. I'm sure the man—Pedro, I presume—wondered what I was doing, but he was very nice about it. He reminded me of someone I have met before but I cannot remember when. But how can that be? I have never been to the Amazon River before, and he certainly didn't look French!"

Disappointed at coming away from Pedro's Place without a clue, Bridget suggested they eat lunch while floating down the river. She opened the drawstring bag and reached in to check out the supplies. After extracting some loaves of bread, some fruit, and candy, Bridget's hand grasped a metal cylinder.

"It's here!" she shouted. "I think the cylinder is in the sack!"

The others gathered around as Bridget pulled a metal cylinder out of the sack, opened it, and extracted a piece of paper, which read:

Clue #5: 16 degrees south latitude and 69 degrees west longitude—Sail the high water and breathe the thin air. Look for a basket, but not for your bread!

"This is kind of spooky," said Bridget. "I keep feeling like Mr. Van Morrow is looking over our shoulders."

"Or someone is," replied Babette. "It is kind of creepy."

"What gives me the creeps is that huge snake on the riverbank," Barnaby exclaimed, looking about 15 feet from the raft's edge.

Beauregard pulled the Coordinator out of the backpack. "It's time to go," he told his friends as he eyed the snake slithering into the river.

✍ QUIZ #6 ✍
Trace the River Basins

1. Define the term river basin.

2. Look at the map of South America on page 48 and list two of the rivers that are part of the Amazon Basin.

3. List three major rivers that merge southward into the Rio de la Plata.

4. Locate a river basin in the region in which you live. What major rivers form the basin?

5. What does it mean when the guidebook says that the Amazon River is the largest river in the world? How does it compare with the Nile River in Africa?

✎ ✎ ✎ ✎ ✎

The main sensation that greeted the questers when their Co-ordinator-induced whirl abated came from the very cool, dry air that surrounded them. They looked around at the snow-covered peaks of the Andes Mountains as they stood on the shore of a large lake.

"This is Lake Titicaca," announced Bridget, who had researched the coordinates before pressing the button on the Coordinator this time. "It is about 120 miles long, 45 miles wide, and 920 feet deep at its deepest point."

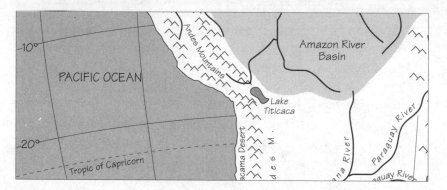

Figure 17: Lake Titicaca

"But you were supposed to set the latitude coordinate at 16 degrees south latitude," said Babette between shivers. "We were 18 degrees north latitude in Montego Bay and it was much warmer there. Sixteen degrees is closer to the equator than 18 degrees!"

"I'm sure I set it correctly," replied Bridget as she checked the machine to make sure. "Those coordinates were meant to take us to Lake Titicaca and here we are," she added defensively.

"The answer is quite simple," interjected Barnaby with an air of scientific superiority. "It all has to do with altitude."

"What do you mean?" Bridget asked.

"**Altitude** is the height of a point on earth above sea level— the average height of the world's ocean water," Barnaby went on. "Lake Titicaca is about 12,500 feet above sea level according to the guidebook, and the temperature can drop 3.5 to 4 degrees Fahrenheit for every 1,000 feet of altitude above sea level."

"So that's why there are mountains near the equator with snow-covered peaks," added Beauregard.

"Exactly," replied Barnaby. "As air rises with higher altitude, it becomes thinner and loses carbon dioxide and water vapor which are heat-retaining elements. The water vapor, is lost by condensation. That's why the area on that side of the mountain range will be wet."

"And the other side of the mountain range will be dry, since the moisture was lost as the air rose," Bridget said.

"Yes," replied Barnaby. "Geography influences the weather of a region."

"All that is very interesting," Babette interjected. "But it is very cold here, no matter what the reason. Let's hurry up and get out of here!"

✍ QUIZ #7 ✍
A Mixed Bag

1. Why is it cooler sitting on a mountain top than walking along a beach?

2. Lake Titicaca (fig. 17, p. 58) is located in the western part of South America, about halfway down the continent. Before reading on, see if you can predict what is so special about this lake.

3. When you see a sign that reads "Jones City, Elevation 582 ft.," what does that mean?

4. In the western United States, there is a city known as "the mile high city." Look in an atlas to see if you can find the city. Hint: A mile is 5,280 feet. How much should the temperature drop from sea level to this city? (Later you will learn that there are factors in addition to altitude that can affect weather.)

✎ ✎ ✎ ✎ ✎

Pulling out the piece of paper again, Bridget said, "High altitude explains the 'thin air'…"

Barnaby squinted to view the objects on the lake in the distance and added, "And it looks like people are sailing on the water."

"But what about those baskets that are not for bread?" questioned Bridget. "I suppose we need to walk around nearer the lake to get some more answers and maybe a cylinder."

A brisk walk toward the lake helped to warm the questers up.

They noticed tall reeds growing in the area, with some thin spots where the reeds had been cut down. Nearing the lake, they came upon a group of people surrounded by stacks of the reeds.

"Look at that!" exclaimed Barnaby as the friends neared the group. "They're using the reeds to make little boats."

The workers greeted Barnaby, Bridget, Babette, and Beauregard and invited them to inspect a boat that was nearly finished. It was shaped somewhat like a canoe, and was big enough for one person and her belongings. One of the workers explained that boats like this had been used to sail on Lake Titicaca since the Incas lived in the area hundreds of years ago.

"Lake Titicaca is the highest navigable lake in the world," stated Bridget as they watched people casting off from the shore in their small boats.

"I don't know if I'd trust one of those boats," said Beauregard as he eyed the tiny craft suspiciously. "I'd feel like I had left shore in a basket."

As soon as the words left his mouth, the four questers looked at each other in amazement.

"Baskets!" said Babette excitedly. "Of course! We need to look in the boats for the next cylinder!"

They spied a group of the craft lined along the shore in the distance. "Let's work in pairs," Barnaby suggested.

Barnaby and Bridget searched in one area while Beauregard and Babette searched in another. Before long, Beauregard dove into one of the small reed boats and surfaced with a shiny cylinder in his paw.

"Got it!" he shouted.

"Quick! Open it and read the clue," said Babette as a cool breeze passed over the water.

The four friends gathered around and read the next clue:

You are "sailing" along in your adventure!   BVM

Clue #6:   53 degrees south latitude and 70 degrees west longitude—Ready for a change of season? You may need an early explorer's cape!

"Do you think the change of season part means that it will be warmer at our next destination?" asked Babette hopefully.

"Fifty-three degrees south latitude...I don't think so," said Barnaby as he consulted the guidebook. "It looks like we're headed for the Tierra del Fuego at the bottom of South America."

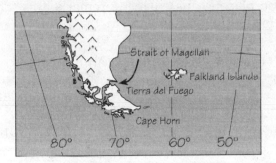

Figure 18: Tierra del Fuego

Barnaby set the Coordinator according to the latitude and longitude points given and asked, "Everyone ready?"

"What time is it?" asked Bridget as she looked around in the darkness.

"Five-thirty in the afternoon," replied Barnaby as he peered at the glowing dial of his watch. "It's never dark this early during summer at home."

"It does not look or feel like summer!" added Babette. "I think it is colder here than it was at Lake Titicaca."

As was becoming his habit, Beauregard was using the first few minutes to check out the new location. He sensed no peril other than the uncomfortable chill, but his nose alerted him to the possibility of a delicious dinner.

"I smell seafood cooking," Beauregard announced to the others as he followed his sensitive nose in the direction of the delectable aroma.

The area was deserted except for the lights from a group of buildings in the distance. "It must be coming from that direction," said Babette. "It looks like a small village."

"Let's go find a place to get in from the cold," Bridget said as she started walking toward the buildings. "Maybe we can find dinner at the same time. Follow your nose, Beauregard!"

Beauregard led his friends into the village and stopped in front of a large square building. "That delectable smell is coming from in here," he informed them.

A small light was shining beside the front door of the building, illuminating a sign which read "Magellan Hotel—Rooms and Meals."

"This is the place for us," Babette remarked as they went into the hotel. Down a short hallway to the right they could see a cozy dining room with a fire.

The questers were greeted by a charming waiter and taken to a table close to the fire. Before long they were eating delicious seafood, vegetables, and rice, followed by a variety of sumptuous desserts.

After dinner, the group approached the clerk at the front desk and requested two rooms.

"We don't get many visitors in the winter," said the desk clerk as he registered the new guests.

"Winter? But it's nearly July!" Bridget exclaimed.

"June 29th to be exact," replied the clerk as he glanced at the calendar. "But I guess you're used to the seasons of the northern hemisphere. You must remember where you are now."

The clerk used a round paperweight to explain his point that the earth tilts on its axis during the year. For part of the year, the northern hemisphere receives more direct sun than the southern hemisphere, and that's when their summer occurs. During the other part of the year, the southern hemisphere receives more direct sun than the northern hemisphere, which is when the southern hemisphere has its warm weather and the northern weather gets colder.

"So our seasons are the reverse of yours in New York," the clerk said after glancing at Bridget's address on the hotel register. "We have winter during June, July, and August, and summer in December, January, and February!"

"So that is why it is dark so early," added Babette as she looked out the window. "Just like it gets dark early in January at home during the winter."

"Now you're thinking along with our seasons," said the desk clerk as he handed the room keys to the questers. "It's cold here on the strait now, so be sure to dress warmly if you plan to visit the cape. The winds are fierce there."

Before they could ask the desk clerk what strait and cape he was talking about, another guest approached the desk to ask if any mail had arrived that day. With their keys in hand, the weary travelers went upstairs to their rooms.

After freshening up a bit, the group met in Bridget and Babette's room to learn more about their location from the guidebook.

"The Tierra del Fuego is actually an archipelago," read Babette, remembering the term from their geography lesson at Montego Bay.

"What about the strait and cape the desk clerk mentioned?" Bridget inquired.

"It says here that a **strait** is a very narrow passage of water that connects two larger bodies of water," replied Babette as she referred to the guidebook. "A **channel** is also a passage of water connecting two larger bodies of water, but a channel is wider than a strait."

"Like the English Channel between England and France," she added.

"Here we are," said Barnaby, pointing to the map. "We're near the Strait of Magellan, which connects the Atlantic and Pacific Oceans."

"And named after the early explorer Ferdinand Magellan, who sailed through here in 1520," added Babette as she read on in the guidebook.

Figure 19: Channel–Strait

"But the clue mentioned an early explorer's cape," said Bridget. "Does the guidebook mention a cape, Babette?"

"Let's see..." replied Babette as she thumbed through the book,

"Yes, here it is—a **cape** is a small point of land, surrounded by water on three sides, which extends out into the sea."

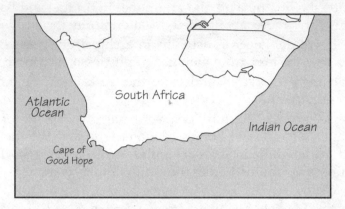

Figure 20: Cape

"Cape Horn is located right near here on Horn Island," said Barnaby as he pointed excitedly to the map. "Cape Horn is at the southern tip of South America."

"I suppose that means we'll have to travel to Cape Horn to look for the next clue," said Beauregard, remembering the desk clerk's talk of cold wind at the cape.

"Let's think about that in the morning," said Bridget. "I'm too tired to look for anything right now."

Goodnights were said and the questers retired to their rooms for some well-deserved sleep.

Beauregard awoke the next morning to find Barnaby sitting straight up in bed, staring at arctic weather clothes piled on a chair on the opposite side of the room.

"Where did those clothes come from?" he asked Beauregard.

Beauregard said he didn't know, but he suspected Bridget may have experienced a burst of predawn energy and decided to get the group ready for a trip to that cold, windy cape.

A moment later there was a knock at the door and Bridget came in excitedly, followed by a sleepy Babette.

"Who put those clothes in our room?" asked Bridget, looking at Barnaby and Beauregard.

"The same person who put those clothes here," replied Barnaby, pointing to the chair.

"Whoever it was is giving us a hint about the temperature in store for us," Babette sighed as she felt the thick down lining of the parkas.

"Let's get dressed and get it over with," said Bridget. "Everything points to finding a clue there."

Barnaby and Beauregard started to dress in their new warm clothes, and Bridget and Babette went off to do the same.

"I can't get my paw through here," thought Beauregard as he pushed at the sleeve of his parka. A couple of minutes later, Barnaby helped him clear the blockage...by removing a shiny cylinder from the parka's sleeve.

Barnaby and Beauregard yelled out to Bridget and Babette, and the questers were soon opening the next cylinder.

"Maybe this means we can forego the journey to the cape," Beauregard said happily as Barnaby unfolded the piece of paper.

Hope you like your new clothes! BVM

Clue #7:   70 degrees south latitude and 0 degrees longitude—The natives are formal, but come as you are. Look for more knowledge at the flashing red light.

"But zero degrees sounds like trouble to me," Babette commented as she set the Coordinator.

✍ QUIZ #8 ✍
Channels, Straits, and Capes

Match the definition with the correct term.

1. A very narrow passage of water that connects two larger bodies of water.

2. A wide passage of water connecting two larger bodies of water.

3. A small point of land, surrounded by water on three sides, that extends into the sea.

4. A group of islands or a body of water containing many islands.

    a. Archipelago

    b. Channel

    c. Strait

    d. Cape

✍ EXERCISE #5 ✍
A Scavenger Hunt...Are You Game?

With a friend, or in a group or in teams, use this book, an atlas, a globe, and any other resource you can find in the library to find the points of longitude and latitude for all the places listed below. The winning group is the one that gets all the answers correct first. (Count the answers as correct if you are within 3 degrees latitude and longitude of the answers given in the back of the book.)

1. Macassar Strait—Near the equator in the South Pacific

2. Mozambique Channel—Between East Africa and Madagascar

3. Karimata Strait—Slightly south of the equator in the Java Sea

4. Bald Head—See the southwest quadrant of Australia

5. Bismarck Archipelago—A few degrees south of the equator in the Bismarck Sea

6. Davis Strait—Toward the North Pole near Baffin Bay

7. Hudson Strait—Locate Hudson Bay in North America

8. Cape Cod—Check 42° N latitude in the Gulf of Maine in North America

9. Yucatan Channel—Slightly above 20° N latitude in North America

10. Cape Hatteras—Check 35° N latitude off the east coast of North America

11. Strait of Magellan—Go to the southern tip of South America

12. Cape Horn—Go to the southern tip of South America

13. Tuamotu Archipelago—In the South Pacific near the International Date Line

14. Tierra del Fuego—Go to the southern tip of South America

15. Cape Sao Roque—Check 5° S latitude of the equator off the eastern coast of South America

16. English Channel—Western Europe, check 50° N latitude near the Strait of Dover

17. Strait of Gibraltar—Between 30 and 40° N latitude between Africa and Europe

18. Saint George's Channel—Near the English Channel in Europe, see the Irish Sea

19. Strait of Messina—Southeastern Europe—38° N latitude near the Mediterranean Sea

20. Strait of Oltranto—Find the Adriatic Sea and the Ionian Sea, Southeastern Europe

21. Bering Strait—At Arctic Circle between North America and Asia

22. Gulf of Tonkin—Search in the South China Sea

23. Palk Strait—Find the Indian Ocean, check near 10° N latitude

24. Strait of Hormuz—Between the Persian Gulf and Gulf of Oman in the Arabian Sea

25. Formosa Strait—Above the Tropic of Cancer in the East China Sea

26. Cape Verde—About 18° N latitude off the coast of Africa

Chapter 5
Antarctica and
the Arctic Regions

The reason for the new winter garments became obvious as soon as the Coordinator delivered them to their new destination. The four explorers found themselves standing on ice, in darkness, with strong gusts of wind whipping the fur on their parka hoods around wildly.

"So this is Antarctica," observed Bridget. "Not exactly inviting, is it?"

"Now I understand why most of the scientists leave here during the winter," Barnaby replied. "It's so cold that their instruments probably freeze."

"Speaking of freezing," replied Bridget, "we'd better get moving before we turn into icicles. But it's so dark—which direction should we take?"

Because cats see so much better in the dark than humans, Beauregard had already spotted a faint red glow blinking in the distance to their left. He pointed out the light to Bridget, Babette, and Barnaby.

"I can't see anything, Beauregard," said Bridget as she squinted into the darkness. "But your nose led us to the right place at the last location, so we'll trust your eyes to do the same this time. Come on, everybody, let's follow Beauregard."

The thick parka hid the degree to which Beauregard's chest puffed importantly as he led the questers across the ice. "It's about time they recognized some of my more unique features," he thought to himself. "If it weren't for me..."

Beauregard's thoughts were interrupted suddenly as the questers found themselves joined by a group of Emperor penguins. The largest penguins were almost the same size as the explorers, and they moved swiftly with their peculiar waddling walk. Beauregard found himself feeling a little peeved with the penguins, since everybody was now staring at them.

"They really do look like they're wearing tuxedos," thought Babette as she walked briskly toward the blinking red light she could now make out ahead of them.

Each blast of frigid air that came gusting across the ice spurred them to walk even faster toward the red light, and they were soon standing in front of a small building. It was a simple structure, built low and sturdy on the ice, with no windows, only a door and the outside light.

"Looks like one of the scientific stations I've seen in journals," thought Barnaby. "The place looks deserted, though."

The penguins stood around the door of the building with the questers, as if waiting for them to do something. So, the questers tried the door. To their surprise, it was unlocked and the inside lights were on—as if someone was expecting them.

The kids and the cat entered the building, and the penguins marched off into the distance.

"I still say this is spooky," said Babette as she noted the wood in the stove all ready to light, and more stacked neatly nearby. "I know Mr. Van Morrow is dead, but it is almost as if someone is shadowing us on this journey."

"That's just your imagination," scoffed Barnaby as he lit the stove. "Everyone said that Mr. Van Morrow was eccentric, and he had the money to plan every little detail."

"Down to a videotaped welcome to Antarctica," added Bridget as she held up a videotape she found on the table titled "For the UNICEF Explorers, from BVM."

Bridget, Barnaby, Babette, and Beauregard gathered around to view the video as the warmth of the fire penetrated the room. They were surprised to be greeted by Mr. Van Morrow himself.

"Hello, I'm Bartholomew Van Morrow...or rather the late Bartholomew Van Morrow by the time you see this video. Welcome to Antarctica! I trust that my old friends, the Emperor penguins, escorted you to the door. They are hardy creatures to be able to survive the winter here—among the few who can.

"Antarctica has no permanent human residents, although thousands of scientists flock here in the summer. If you are unfortunate enough to be here during the winter, you will find it a lonely place indeed. However, just being here means that you are well on your way to learning more about our earth and its geography. Although I have traveled all over the world, I have a special interest in the polar regions, so would like to tell you about them myself.

"You are now at 70 degrees south latitude, but still quite a distance from the South Pole. The poles of the earth are located at 90 degrees south and north latitude. By now, you know that the equator is at 0 degrees latitude and that the sun's rays hit in a direct line with the equator. You should also have learned that, due to the tilting of the earth during its rotation around the sun every year, the northern and southern hemispheres experience summer and winter at opposite times of the year.

"Since the poles are located at 90 degrees latitude away from the equator, the sun's rays do not hit at a direct angle, even in the summer. In fact, during the summer—December and January at the South Pole and June and July at the North Pole—the sun's rays are visible twenty-four hours a day due to the earth's tilt. Conversely, the same tilt that makes one pole experience summer daylight for twenty-four hours a day during summer will plunge the opposite pole into twenty-four hours of darkness during its winter months. If you are here during the Antarctic winter, you will have arrived here in darkness regardless of the time of day."

Barnaby glanced at his watch. Despite the darkness outside, it read 11 a.m. "It's wintertime here, all right," he thought.

Mr. Van Morrow was now pointing to maps of the Antarctic and Arctic regions:

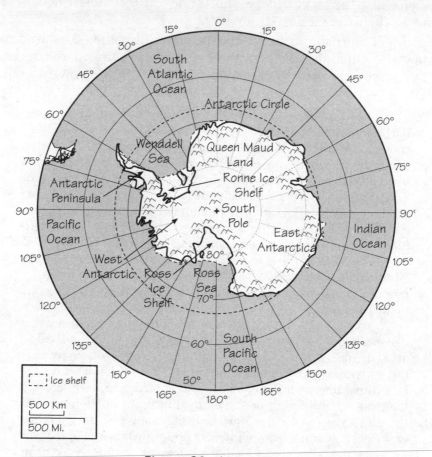

Figure 21: Antarctica

"You will notice the Arctic Circle and the Antarctic Circle on these maps. These circles mark the point at which the sun stays above the horizon for at least one 24-hour period during the year—the 'Land of the Midnight Sun,' as some call it.

"It may sound as if the Arctic and Antarctic regions are similar but actually, they are quite different. Let me explain. The Arctic region is basically an ocean surrounded by three continents. This ocean, the Arctic Ocean, is the smallest of the world's oceans and is frozen over the North Pole. However, the Arctic is about 35 degrees Fahrenheit warmer than the Antarctic due to warming ocean currents, and some of the ice breaks up to form moving packs during the summer. There are permanent human residents within the Arctic Circle and a variety of wildlife—polar bears, reindeer, caribou, wolves—can also be found there.

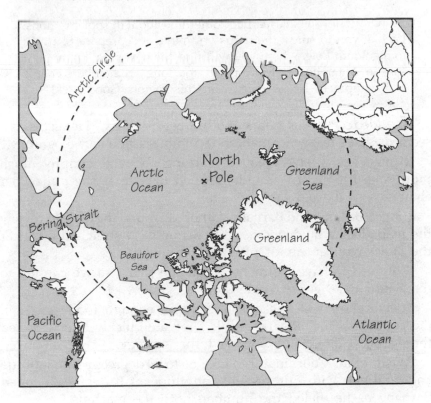

Figure 22: The Arctic Region

"Antarctica is a continent surrounded by three oceans. The continent may seem bigger than it actually is because of the formation of ice shelves at its edge. An ice shelf may be up to 3 miles thick and may never completely melt, although icebergs may break off from time to time. These icebergs can cause havoc to ships in the polar regions. You will see ice everywhere in Antarctica—in fact, 90 percent of the earth's fresh water can be found in the ice here!

"Antarctica has an average altitude of 6,000 feet, and there are mountains on this continent as high as 15,000 feet."

"Just what the place needs," thought Beauregard as he felt a nap coming on with the encroaching warmth of the fire, "a higher altitude to make it even colder." He took off his parka and lay down next to the stove.

The video of Mr. Van Morrow continued:

> "Now that you have learned something about the polar regions, I'd like you to study the maps you have and prepare to travel to the South Pole, where you will find the next clue. Enjoy your stay in Antarctica, but don't stay too long—remember, people and equipment freeze quickly in this region. Good luck!"

The video screen went dark and Bridget observed, "He seems...er, seemed...like a really nice man, and so enthusiastic about geography."

"I must say, I have enjoyed learning about geography much more than I thought I would," replied Babette as she pulled her chair nearer the old table.

Bridget, Babette, and Barnaby gathered around the table to review the maps in the guidebook, while Beauregard stretched out near the stove with an air of utter contentment.

"We need to have a strategy," Babette said, "so we can get to the South Pole, get the clue, and be gone."

After a short rest, the questers found enough food stored in the cupboards for a hearty meal. They ate quickly, then donned their arctic clothes and reviewed the strategy.

"We'll set the Coordinator to take us to 90 degrees south latitude and continue with our present longitude of 0 degrees," stated Barnaby as he dialed the numbers into the machine.

"We all need to look for the cylinder, but stay close together in case a blizzard hits," reminded Bridget. "In a blizzard, we couldn't see each other even a few feet away."

They all held the Coordinator as Babette pushed the button. Their next sensation was struggling to stay upright in the face of a strong wind blowing relentlessly across an expanse of ice. The wind made moving around in search of the cylinder more difficult than the questers had imagined.

"I've heard the winds in Antarctica can reach 200 miles per hour," Barnaby remembered as he peered about for a metallic cylinder.

Finally, Babette spotted a signpost that read "The South Pole," and something metallic glimmering beneath it. Digging quickly, she extracted the cylinder, which held their next clue.

"Hurry," shouted Bridget. "I'm afraid the Coordinator is going to freeze up. Remember what Mr. Van Morrow said about people and equipment freezing here!"

Babette made her way back to Bridget and Barnaby with the cylinder, and they quickly read the next clue:

Welcome to the bottom of the world!   BVM

Clue #8: 25 degrees south latitude and 132 degrees east longitude—Check your watch as you look for rocks. Much more of the same is buried underground.

"Hey, where's Beauregard?" shouted Babette, realizing they all needed to be holding on to the Coordinator before leaving the South Pole.

The wind had proven too much even for a cat of Beauregard's size. He had been knocked down and was lying flat on his back, looking something like a large, frozen penguin.

"Quick, set the machine!" shouted Babette as she ran over to Beauregard. Babette was amazingly strong. She dragged Beauregard over the ice in a manner which in any other circumstance would have been severely embarrassing for him. This was hardly a time to care about appearances, however.

Bridget knew there was no time to check the location of their next destination. "Let's hope it's a dry, safe landing," she thought, as they all bent down to make sure Beauregard's paws were on the machine.

✍ QUIZ #9 ✍
True or False

Say whether the following statements are true or false.

1. Antarctica has no permanent human residents.

2. The poles of the earth are located at 75 degrees south and north latitude.

3. The equator is at 0 degrees latitude, and the sun's rays hit in a direct line with the equator.

4. Due to the tilting of the earth during its rotation around the sun every year, the northern and southern hemispheres experience summer and winter at opposite times of the year.

5. Because the poles are located at 90 degrees latitude away from the equator, the sun's rays do not hit at a direct angle, even in the summer.

6. During the summer months—December and January at the South Pole, and June and July at the North Pole—the sun's rays are visible twenty-four hours a day due to the earth's tilt.

7. The same tilt that gives one pole daylight for twenty-four hours a day during summer plunges the opposite pole into darkness for twenty-four hours a day during winter.

8. The Arctic Circle and the Antarctic Circle mark the point at which the sun stays above the horizon for at least one twenty-four-hour period during the year.

9. The Arctic and Antarctic are often referred to as the "Land of the All Day Sun."

10. The arctic region is basically an ocean surrounded by three continents.

11. The Arctic Ocean is the smallest of the world's oceans and is frozen over the North Pole.

12. The Arctic is about 35 degrees Fahrenheit warmer than the Antarctic due to warming ocean currents.

13. There are permanent human residents within the Arctic Circle, as well as a variety of wildlife including polar bears, reindeer, caribou, and wolves.

14. Antarctica is a continent surrounded by four oceans.

15. Antarctica may seem bigger than it actually is because of the formation of ice shelves at its edge.

16. An ice shelf may be up to three miles thick and may never completely melt.

17. Icebergs can cause havoc to ships in the polar regions.

18. Seventy-five percent of the earth's fresh water can be found in the ice cap covering Antarctica.

19. Antarctica has an average altitude of 6,000 feet and has mountains.

20. There are mountains on Antarctica that reach an altitude of 15,000 feet.

✍ EXERCISE #6 ✎
A Trip to the South Pole

1. Pretend that you are preparing to take a trip to the antarctic region. Describe and compare what you would take with you in summer as compared to winter. Don't think only of clothes.

2. Try the following experiment with a friend. Find a globe about the size of a basketball (in fact, a basketball or soccer ball will do fine) and a regular flashlight. Go into a darkened room and prepare for the experiment. Hold the flashlight straight in front of you about chest high. Have your friend move about 5 feet away from you and hold the globe with the poles placed straight up and down. Shine the flashlight on the globe. Notice that the direct light hits the globe right in the middle, at the equator.

Without moving the flashlight, have your friend tilt the north, or top, pole toward you 23.5 degrees. To do this, imagine the North Pole straight up is at the 12 o'clock position on a clock—your friend should move the North Pole toward you to the 1 o'clock position—a slight tilt.

Chapter 6
Oceania and World Time Zones

"Whew!" Babette thought as she felt her feet land on solid ground at their new destination. "A dry landing...I wonder if it is safe, too."

She opened her eyes to see the last colors of a sunset fading into night over an expanse of flat land. There was an outline of what seemed to be a mountain in the distance, and the questers appeared to be the only people around.

"Where do you think we are?" Barnaby asked, looking about.

"We need to look up the coordinates on the map," replied Babette, "and that is not possible now that it is dark."

Beauregard, having landed lying down this time, rapidly got to his feet. He returned to normal quickly and, using his excellent feline vision, soon spotted a few pieces of wood near some brush for a campfire. It wasn't long before the explorers had collected enough material for a fire.

"It's ready to light," announced Bridget proudly as she surveyed the strategically built pile of wood and sticks.

"That may be a problem if we do not have matches," responded Babette as she realized their current dilemma. "Perhaps we could try rubbing sticks together?"

The four friends stared at the unlit pile of sticks, trying to think of possible solutions. As he often did when pondering possibilities,

Barnaby began scratching his head. Sure enough, within a few seconds, there was a clunk on the ground.

"What was that?" asked Babette, looking at the ground.

Beauregard spotted the shiny object that had fallen from Barnaby's hair and held it up to catch what little light was available from the moon.

"It looks like a lighter—a barbecue lighter!" Bridget exclaimed.

"Oh, I accused someone of losing that during a cookout last May!" said Barnaby as he took the lighter and lit the pile of sticks and wood.

Soon the questers were settled around a glowing campfire that warded off the night chill.

"We're in Australia!" announced Babette as she located their coordinates on the map, "and it looks like we are almost in the middle of the continent."

"The guidebook says that Australia is the flattest of the continents," she continued. "The land around here certainly looks that way, except for that mountain or whatever it is in the distance."

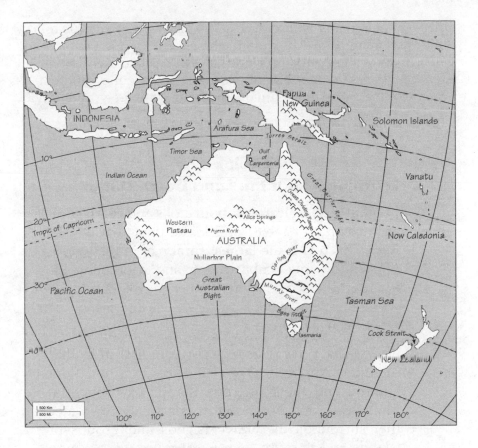

Figure 23: Australia, New Zealand, Oceania

"What else does it say about Australia?" asked Barnaby as he stretched out beside Beauregard, who was already napping beside the campfire.

"That Australia is also the smallest, lowest, and driest of the continents, " Babette replied. "Australia is quite dry west of the Great Dividing Range, but **artesian water** can be found in some places."

"What kind of water is that?" asked Bridget.

Babette read on: "It is underground water that rises to form a spring whenever there is a crack in the earth's surface. It is salty, however, so is used mainly to support sheep, rather than as drinking water for humans.

"Australia is often included with New Zealand and Oceania

whenever geography is discussed. Oceania is a region 8,000 miles wide, stretching from Australia to the central Pacific Ocean, and is made up of thousands of islands. New Zealand has two main islands and lies to the east of Australia. It is quite different—because of the moist, mild climate, the islands are green and hilly."

✍ EXERCISE #7 ✍
Learning About the Land Down Under

1. In chapter 3 you learned about atolls and coral. Look at the map on page 81 and locate the Great Barrier Reef. This reef is the largest coral reef in the world. Look into some scuba diving and snorkeling literature to discover why thousands of divers go there. Check out a book on coral reefs and see where others can be found.

2. Oceania is a more recent term for the area that includes Australia, New Zealand, Papua New Guinea, and the numerous islands of Melanesia, Micronesia, and Polynesia. It is actually the water that surrounds the above islands and groups of islands and is more than 8,000 miles wide. There are literally thousands of islands in Oceania. Plan an imaginary trip to a group of the smaller islands, perhaps French Polynesia. You could visit Tahiti and check out the Tuamotu Archipelago. What would you need on your visit? What would you wear and what would you do there? Hint: Better talk to Babette and brush up on your French. *Au revoir!*

3. List ten facts about the land and the continent of Australia. How does Australia compare to New Zealand?

4. Do you remember the continental divide in North America from chapter 2? If not, go back and review or check out the map on page 23. Then, look at

the map of Australia on page 81 and see if you can determine where the continental divide is located there. Into what ocean(s) do the Murray and Darling Rivers flow?

✎ ✎ ✎ ✎ ✎

"What time is it?" asked Bridget as she stretched the next morning.

"More like what day is it!" exclaimed Babette. "We have been in such a whirl going from place to place with the Coordinator, I no longer know what day it is!"

"What day and time it is depends on where you are," Beauregard stated as he handed Babette the guidebook opened to a page headed "Time Zones."

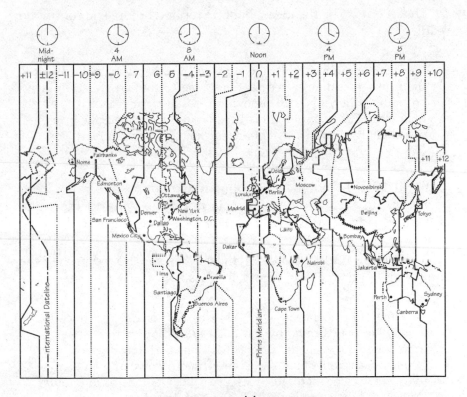

Figure 24: World time zones

It seemed that Beauregard had been doing some early morning research while the others were still asleep by the campfire. The book showed a map of the world divided into sections that resembled longitudinal lines, but appeared as odd shapes in some places. Babette took the guidebook and read to the others:

"As the earth rotates, some parts of the world have sunlight while other parts are in darkness. Instead of having part of the world experience darkness at 9 a.m. while another part has sunlight at 9 a.m., the earth is divided into **twenty-four time zones**— one time zone for each hour of the day. By having time zones, sunrise occurs at approximately the same time—6 a.m.—all over the world."

"So when it's noon, the sun should be at midpoint at that part of the world," Barnaby added.

"That seems to be the idea," Babette replied before she continued reading:

"The beginning of the time zones is at 0 degrees longitude— the prime meridian. For each time zone to the left (west), it is an hour earlier; for each time zone to the right (east), it is an hour later. For example, if it is 12 noon in London near the prime meridian, it would be five hours earlier, or 7 a.m., in New York City, which is five time zones to the left, or west."

"So, if it is 12 noon in London, it would be one hour later, or 1 p.m., in Cape Town, which is one time zone to the right, or east," Bridget said slowly as she was figuring out the time zones.

"So it would seem," Babette remarked as she looked at the time zone map. "Let me see what else it says:

"Time zones continue until 180 degrees longitude, which is exactly halfway around the earth. At this point, there are twelve time zones between the prime meridian and 180 degrees longitude. Specifically, half of the time zones (twelve of the twenty-four) are located here, just as half of the degrees of longitude (180 of the 360) are here. The point of 180 degrees longitude is called the **International Date Line**—the point at which one day ends and another begins. The other twelve time zones continue until the prime meridian is reached to complete the circle. Most time zones are 15 degrees of longitude wide. So, at the equator a time zone is basically 69 miles x 15 degrees, for a total of 1,035 miles. Time zones do not go straight (fig. 24, p. 83) or curve like the meridians of longitude. The lines are drawn for political, geographical, or convenience reasons."

"I remember going on a trip to California once," exclaimed Bridget. "We took a southern route down to see my aunt in Atlanta. We were still in the same time zone as my friends in New York, which was Eastern Standard Time. When we left Georgia and traveled to Alabama we entered Central Standard Time. Then we went west to Texas and entered Central Time, then to New Mexico and Mountain Standard Time. Once we passed through New Mexico and Arizona, we hit the border of California and entered Pacific Standard Time."

"Well, that is one reason why state boundaries are not straight lines, but that isn't the case for every state" Beauregard mumbled to himself, thinking of South Carolina. "Anyway, what's the big deal? You can only be in one place at a time."

"There doesn't seem to be much around the International Date Line except the Pacific and Arctic Oceans," Barnaby observed.

"That's part of the plan," Babette responded as she referred to the guidebook. "If the International Date Line fell between New York City and Chicago, think of the confusion there would be with the United States straddling two days on the calendar! With the International Date Line where it is, a lot of confusion is avoided."

"What are the shaded areas on the map?" Bridget asked.

"The book says that these are called Irregular Time Zones. They differ from other time zones by half an hour instead of a full hour," Babette replied. "In addition, some countries modify their time standards to meet their needs."

"Like when we go on Daylight Saving Time in the United States," Barnaby said. "Travelers have to keep all this in mind as they go from place to place."

"We've been zipping in and out of so many time zones," Bridget said. "I guess we'd better keep that in mind if we're to meet the deadline. Which reminds me, hadn't we better look at the clue again so we can start searching for the cylinder?"

✍ QUIZ #10 ✍
Time Zones

Try your luck with these brain teasers. Pretend it is 12 noon on the prime meridian, 0 degrees longitude. What time will it be at each of the places listed below? Just for fun, try to add the continents. Use figure 24 on page 83 to assist you.

<u>City</u>   <u>Time</u>   <u>Continent</u>

1. New York City

2. Berlin

3. Nome

4. Edmonton

5. Novosibirsk

6. San Francisco

7. Honolulu

8. Madrid

9. Nairobi

10. Tokyo

11. Dakar

12. Santiago

13. Mexico City

14. Oslo

15. Beijing

16. Sydney

17. Jakarta

18. Cape Town

19. Moscow

20. Buenos Aires

✍ EXERCISE #8 ✍
Globetrotters' Challenges

1. If one degree of longitude at the equator is roughly 69 miles and there are (theoretically) 15 degrees between each time zone, how would you determine the number of miles around the earth at the equator? How many miles did you get?

2. Would the time zones be affected as you move to 75 degrees north or south latitude? If so, how would they be affected?

✎ ✎ ✎ ✎ ✎

"The clue talked about looking for rocks, and I don't think we'll find one bigger than that," said Beauregard as he pointed into the distance.

Indeed, what had seemed like a mountain in the darkness when the questers arrived was clearly not a mountain, but one huge rock! Bridget, Babette, and Barnaby stared at the stone in amazement.

"Wow!" cried Barnaby excitedly. He grabbed the guidebook, and was soon reading to the others. "It's called Ayers Rock, and it is 1,140 feet high and 2 miles long—the largest monolith or single stone in the world. It also says that only 5 percent of the rock is above the ground!"

"Incredible!" exclaimed Bridget as she tried to imagine the size of the entire rock. "That must be the rock the clue is talking about, so let's go!"

As the questers traveled toward Ayers Rock, they passed some people called Aborigines, the native people of Australia. After exchanging pleasantries, the adventurers continued on toward the rock.

"The guidebook said that the Aborigines consider Ayers Rock to be sacred," Barnaby informed Bridget, Babette, and Beauregard. "so we'd better be careful how we act."

"Yes," Babette replied, staring at the rock that loomed above them. "And we've got a lot of rock to cover in order to find a cylinder!"

"I don't see a trail or anything that would get us up on the rock," observed Barnaby. "So why don't we spread out a little to look in this area. If you see anything, whistle, okay?"

"Sounds workable to me," said Bridget. "We've got to start looking someplace."

Bridget, Babette, Barnaby, and Beauregard spread out in search of a cylinder, each targeting a section of the rock, but keeping within hearing distance of each other.

Beauregard ambled along his designated section and gazed up at the expanse of red sandstone. "That book couldn't have been right in saying this is only 5 percent of the rock," he thought to himself. "Surely, no rock is *that* big."

He ambled along a bit further until he spotted a small area of soil at the rock's edge that looked quite soft, as though it had just been plowed. He had an idea.

"Why don't I dig down a bit to see if this rock really does continue below the surface," he thought as he prepared his claws for some action.

Since Beauregard was a rather large cat, his claws, being in perfect proportion with the rest of his body, enabled him to dig very quickly. Before long, a huge cloud of red dust rose into the air as Beauregard dug faster and faster at the edge of Ayers Rock. Bridget, Barnaby, and Babette were soon on the scene to see what was going on. Beauregard, oblivious to their arrival, continued his search for the bottom of the rock.

Suddenly, his claws hit something hard, but smoother than the sandstone rock. On closer inspection, Beauregard realized he had uncovered the next metal cylinder. Triumphantly, he crawled out of the hole in order to whistle to the others.

Bridget, Babette, and Barnaby stared at Beauregard in amazement. Covered from head to toe in red dust, the only three things that shone forth from that apparition were the cat's eyes and the metal cylinder. "Congratulations, Beauregard!" they cried.

The quester's glee, however, was suddenly interrupted by a rumbling sound coming toward them from the distance.

"Uh-oh," said Barnaby as he looked at the source of the sound. "It's a group of Aborigines, and they're coming straight for us. It sounds like they're chanting 'Uluru, Uluru.' I don't know what that means, but they sure don't look very happy with us. We'd better get out of here—fast!"

Babette was already in combat pose, as was her habit on such occasions, but it was pretty obvious the questers were badly outnumbered. "Quick!" she yelled at Bridget. "Make a balloon!"

Bridget had already begun chewing her bubble gum furiously. In no time, she had a balloon ready for their escape. Bridget, Barnaby, and Babette jumped on board. Beauregard, who was busy with the latch of the cylinder, suddenly found himself hanging by the tail in mid-air. "Just hold on to that cylinder, Beauregard!" yelled Babette, as she began to yank him on board. Although his tail hurt, Beauregard sighed with relief as he looked down at the angry mob gathering below.

"Well, I guess the Aborigines didn't appreciate Beauregard digging at a sacred site," Barnaby exclaimed.

"At least I found the cylinder," said Beauregard defensively as he pulled out the next clue.

Four continents down, three to go! BVM

Clue #9: 23.5 degrees north latitude and 90 degrees east longitude—You'll wish for umbrellas and boots. Monsoons mean hiking to higher ground!

"Why does foul weather seem to go with learning about geography?" sighed Babette as she remembered that a monsoon brought heavy rains.

"It looks like we're headed to Asia," reported Bridget as she placed the coordinates on the map. "That will be our fifth continent, and it looks like we might make the deadline if we keep up this pace—and stay out of trouble."

✍ EXERCISE #9 ✍
Checking Out Rocks

1. Ayers Rock, or Uluru, is quite a rock. How did Ayers Rock get its shape?

2. Ask your librarian to help you find some books on rock formations. What are the three major types of rocks? How are they formed?

3. Investigate how the Himalaya Mountains in Asia were formed.

4. How do the Rocky Mountains and the Appalachian Mountains in North America differ?

Chapter 7
Asia, Deltas, and Climate Zones

Barnaby felt the mud ooze up around his feet and the rain pelt down on him as he steadied himself by clutching on to Beauregard. Beauregard, already going into shock at the thought of being soaked again, held on to his temper while Barnaby held on to him. "If I fall over…" Beauregard thought to himself, "we're both going down."

Finally, the questers were standing upright but, yes, they were soaked through. Beauregard and Barnaby, the ones with the most hair, looked all small again without the extra plumage.

"Mr. Van Morrow was right—we sure could use some umbrellas and boots right now," sighed Barnaby, still steadying himself against Beauregard.

Beauregard didn't say a word. He looked rather like someone trying to keep his temper. He shook Barnaby off.

"Let's see if we can get out of the rain by going to that village over there," suggested Bridget as she pointed to a cluster of small buildings nearby.

The four gallant explorers said little as they walked toward the village, leaping over puddles to avoid slipping in the mud. The downpour was so heavy that small streams had begun to form, connecting the puddles. When they arrived at the village, the residents were in a flurry of activity. Mothers were rounding up their children, fathers were loading the backs of donkeys with bundles, and grandparents went in and out of the houses, carrying belongings to carts.

"The water's rising quickly," an older man explained to the adventurers as they came to one of the homes. "Get as many of your possessions as you can and go to higher ground."

"We just arrived here, and this is our only possession right now," replied Bridget as she indicated the backpack. "But we'll help out."

"That would be very kind of you," said the man, smiling at Bridget. "The rain will soon flood this area, and we need to move as much as we can quickly before it's washed away."

Bridget, Barnaby, Babette, and Beauregard joined the villagers in packing the carts. As the rain continued, the families began to guide the loaded donkeys and carts along a narrow road with the assistance of the four questers.

Babette walked alongside the man they had met on arriving in the village. "Where are we going?" she asked, peering up the road for signs of a destination.

"There's a village farther up the road, on higher ground," the man replied. "Most of these people have relatives who live there and will stay with them until the flooding stops."

"Do you have relatives there, too?" inquired Babette, afraid that the man wouldn't have anywhere to stay at the other village.

"Oh, I live there," responded the man, smiling at Babette's concern. "My name is Zinaur. I traveled down to the lower village early this morning to help some of my relatives in case flooding occurred. Such flooding has happened there before."

After several hours, the caravan arrived at the neighboring village. The rain continued, but the higher area appeared to be safe from flooding.

"You've been so kind to help us," Zinaur said as he turned to Bridget, Barnaby, Babette, and Beauregard after everyone had taken their carts and donkeys off to their relatives' homes. "Please come to my house for shelter and dry clothing. I would be honored if you would join me for dinner, also."

The thought of dry clothing and a meal sounded great to the drenched, tired travelers, and they graciously accepted Zinaur's invitation and followed him home. Beauregard, of course, wasn't so much interested in dry clothing as a nice, cozy spot to lie down. The only good thing about the rain, as far as he was concerned, was that it had washed away the red dust he'd gathered during his dig at Ayers Rock.

"We'll rest here while dinner is being prepared," suggested Zinaur as he motioned to an area scattered with large floor pillows. The kids, now in dry clothing, and Beauregard, with a big towel around his neck, eagerly complied. They sank down into the soft pillows.

"You said flooding had occurred with the rains before, Zinaur," observed Babette. "Does this happen often?"

"Too often, it seems," Zinaur responded. "It is a result of where we live and our climate."

Noting the puzzled expressions on his guests' faces, Zinaur continued:

"We live in southern Asia where the Ganges, Brahmaputra, and three other rivers flow into the Indian Ocean's Bay of Bengal.

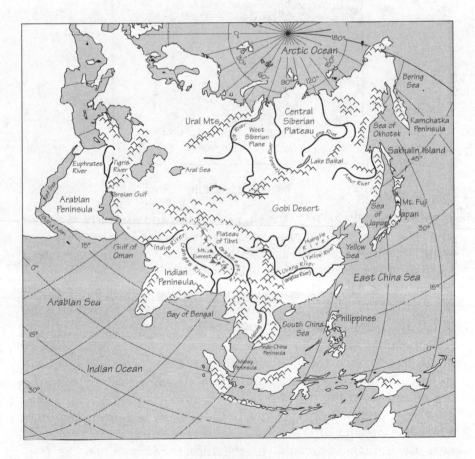

Figure 25: Asia

As a river flows toward the ocean, it brings along sediment consisting of mud and small rocks. The swift current of the river can carry the sediment downstream. However, as the river flow slows as it nears the ocean, the sediment separates out from the water and forms a muddy area of new land. A large pile of new land at the river's mouth, called a delta, forces the river to flow around the piles of earth in smaller streams called distributaries.

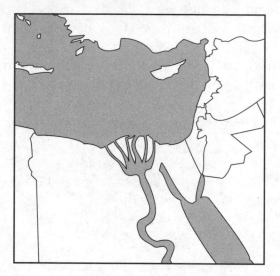

Figure 26: Delta

Deltas usually assume the shape of a fan and are formed where one large river or several merged rivers meet the ocean. The low-lying land of a delta is easily flooded with heavy rains or ocean storms, which bring high tides."

"Before we arrived here we were told to expect a monsoon. A monsoon is a heavy rainstorm, right?" asked Barnaby as he noted the steady downpour outside the house.

"**Monsoons** are actually seasonal winds," replied Zinaur. "Areas of the world at a low latitude that lie along a coastline facing the equator may experience these winds. The winds in the summer, warm and from the direction of the equator, come in from over the ocean, bringing heavy rains. In the winter, the winds originate from the opposite direction, over land, and bring dry air. We are near the Indian Peninsula, or the Indian Subcontinent as it is sometimes called. The ocean current around the Indian Peninsula also alternates direction from summer to winter, because it is influenced by the monsoon winds. These monsoon winds bring some of the heaviest rainfall on earth to this area during the summer months."

"So you have flooding every summer with the rains?" Bridget asked.

"The **floods** are worse some years than others," Zinaur responded, "especially if an ocean storm also occurs. You see, ocean waves are caused by winds over the ocean, and with strong storm winds, the waves can get very high. Whenever a storm occurs in the ocean, like a cyclone in the Indian Ocean, these high waves can easily flood our low-lying coastline, especially during times of high tide. Thousands of our people died in the floods several years ago when an ocean storm and heavy rains caused a particularly bad flood."

"I did not realize it could get that severe," remarked Babette quietly, as she thought of all of the families leaving their village earlier in the day.

"Yes, it can," Zinaur said solemnly. "Floods can occur quickly, before there is time to escape. We have to accept this as part of what comes with living here in this climate."

"We've been traveling quite a bit lately," Barnaby said, "and we've found that weather and climate vary greatly."

"Most of it too wet, too hot, or too cold," Beauregard thought to himself in a sleepy haze, as he snuggled further down into his huge pillow.

"That is so true, my friend," responded Zinaur as he poured tea for his guests. "Climate and weather certainly present some challenges when traveling or living in different parts of the world."

"What's the difference between climate and weather?" asked Bridget as she sipped her tea.

"Weather may change from day to day—rain, sunshine, clouds," replied Zinaur, "but an area's climate is its average weather over a long period of time. The climate of a particular region is influenced by many factors."

"Like altitude," added Babette. "When we were at Lake Titicaca in South America, we learned that the temperature drops 3 to 4 degrees Fahrenheit for every 1,000 feet of altitude above sea level."

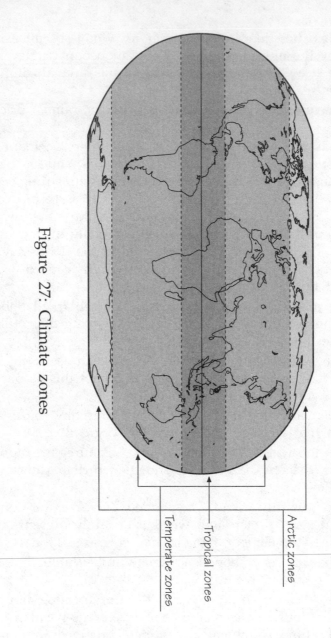

Figure 27: Climate zones

Temperate zones

Tropical zones

Arctic zones

"And that air currents lose moisture as they climb in altitude at a mountain range," interjected Barnaby. "This side of the mountain, called the windward side, receives the heaviest rainfall," he said, gesturing with his hands. "The other side of the mountain, called the leeward or sheltered side, is usually dry since the air has lost most or all of its moisture."

"We've also learned that the activities of humans, such as destroying rain forests and burning fossil fuels, can increase the amount of carbon dioxide in the atmosphere," contributed Bridget. "This excess carbon dioxide can result in a worldwide warming trend or 'greenhouse effect' that can influence many climates."

"You are all quite correct!" exclaimed Zinaur, impressed with his guests' knowledge.

"What else can influence climate?" inquired Bridget.

"Quite a few things," Zinaur continued. "First of all, the earth can be divided into three basic climate zones based on latitude: tropical, temperate, and polar. The sun's rays hit directly on the equator; thus, the tropical zones receive the most heat from the sun, creating a continuous summer.

"The angle and amount of sunshine received by the temperate zones depends on the tilt of the earth at a particular time of the year—more in the summer, less in the winter. The temperate zones are the only ones which experience a change of seasons. The polar regions receive the least amount of sunlight, and the sunlight is always at an angle. This results in cold temperatures throughout the year. Climate can vary, however, within these zones designated by latitude, due to some additional factors.

"Large bodies of water are cooler than land during warm periods and warmer than land during cool periods. The proximity of land to a large body of water, like an ocean or large lake, may determine how warm the land area is in winter and how cool it is in summer. Areas further inland will experience greater extremes."

"Couldn't an ocean current also warm an area?" inquired Babette. "We have learned how the Gulf Stream current of the North Atlantic Ocean flows to Ireland, Great Britain, and western Europe and brings warmer temperatures to those areas."

"Yes, you're quite right," Zinaur responded. "The climates of other areas of the world are influenced by ocean currents as well. For example, southwestern Alaska experiences a warmer climate due to the Northern Pacific Ocean currents. Likewise, the cooler ocean currents and winds of the West Wind Drift current in the southern hemisphere bring cool, dry weather to the southwestern coasts of Africa, South America, and Australia."

"These West Wind Drift ocean winds contribute to the cool, dry climate," Barnaby stated. "But winds can also bring precipitation like the monsoon rains or warmer weather, too, right?"

"Exactly," replied Zinaur. "Another example of the way prevailing winds can influence climate is found along the northwestern coast of the United States, where Pacific winds bring heavy precipitation and cool temperatures."

The questers listened attentively as Zinaur continued, "Mountains can influence land temperatures as well. High mountains can shield southern regions of continents in the northern hemisphere from the invasion of polar air masses during the winter. The alps protect cold snaps from reaching southern Europe, while the Himalayas protect our region of southern Asia. Unfortunately, the low altitude of the Appalachian Mountains fails to stop arctic blasts from reaching the southeastern United States, which sometimes results in subfreezing winter temperatures there."

"I hear about pressure systems on the TV weather reports at home," Babette said. "Does geography have anything to do with these systems?"

"That is the last factor influencing climate," responded Zinaur. "Low pressure atmospheric areas rise, resulting in condensation and precipitation. The subpolar areas and an area along the equator called the doldrums are the two major low pressure belts on earth. The doldrums region averages 70 to 80 inches of precipitation a year, while the subpolar region, located between 45 and 55 degrees north or south latitude, averages 40 to 50 inches of precipitation a year. The areas of the earth where cold polar air meets warm equatorial air are often stormy as areas of pressure collide."

"That sounds like the middle of the United States where storms spawn tornadoes," Barnaby said, as he thought of the latitude position of the area.

"You're thinking just like a geography student!" laughed Zinaur as dinner was brought in.

During dinner, the questers told Zinaur about their mission for the United Nations and UNICEF. He listened carefully, and after the meal he excused himself and went off into another room. A minute later, much to the surprise of his guests, he returned carrying a shiny cylinder.

"Two days ago a man delivered this to my house," Zinaur explained. "He said that visitors on a mission for the United Nations would soon be arriving in the village, and that I should give this metal tube to them. I must say that I was expecting an older delegation!"

The group smiled at each other as Bridget said, "We understand your surprise, but we'll get the job done."

"That is evidenced by the knowledge of geography you have gained already," Zinaur replied. "I wish you well as you continue on your mission."

A while later, as the adventurers were settling down to a good night's rest, Bridget thought of what Zinaur had said about the delivery of the cylinder to his home. "I'm beginning to see what you mean about feeling like we're being watched," she whispered to Babette in the darkness.

✍ QUIZ #11 ✍
Climate and Weather

1. Trace and list the two rivers that flow into the Indian Ocean's Bay of Bengal. (See fig. 28, p. 101.)

2. What is a delta and how is it formed? Draw a picture of the delta that is formed in North America as the Mississippi River flows into the Atlantic Ocean's Gulf of Mexico. (See fig. 4, p. 23.)

3. Monsoons are seasonal winds. How do they bring heavy rains which can cause flooding?

4. Floods can be made worse by ocean storms. How does an ocean storm start?

5. Describe the difference between climate and weather?

6. Why does the windward side of a mountain receive more rainfall than the leeward side?

7. How can the greenhouse effect influence climate? What can people do about this problem?

✍ EXERCISE #10 ☜
The Weather

1. Design a presentation for your class or your friends showing how latitude, the earth's tilt, bodies of water, ocean currents, prevailing winds, mountains, and atmospheric pressure define the three climate zones: tropical, temperate, and polar. (see fig. 27, p. 96.)

2. With a group of friends or classmates, design a weather program and videotape a simulated broadcast of the weather on a specific date in specific locations in each of the three climate zones. Be sure to include the area where you live.

✎ ✎ ✎ ✎ ✎

The next morning, the four explorers thanked Zinaur for his exceptional hospitality, said good-bye and good luck, and went out into the early morning sunshine. Babette opened the new cylinder. It read:

Are you dried out and ready to go again? BVM

Clue #10: 27.5 degrees north latitude and 87 degrees east longitude—Get out the coats and lift your spirits. You'll soon be on top of the world!

"The last clue was certainly right about needing umbrellas and boots," observed Beauregard. "Let's get out the coats before we travel this time."

"Good idea," said Bridget as she pulled their cold-weather gear out of the backpack.

After donning their gloves and zipping their parkas, the travelers set the Coordinator for their next destination.

"Wow! Would you look at these mountains!" exclaimed Barnaby as the group found themselves standing in the middle of the tallest mountain range they had ever seen. The white, bright snow on the slopes of the mountains almost blinded them as they looked around.

"The coordinates indicate that we are in the Himalayas," Babette notified the others after looking up the guidebook.

Figure 28: Bay of Bengal

"And if the temperature is any indication, we must be at a very high altitude," added Beauregard, feeling pleased with himself for having suggested the cold-weather clothing before arriving at their current destination.

To their surprise, the new arrivals to the Himalayas saw quite a lot of activity nearby, at a group of tents. A cold blast of air coming down the slope encouraged them to begin walking toward the shelter of the camp.

As they entered the campsite they were greeted with curious but friendly looks from other parka-clad people. As Babette nodded hello to one person, she quickly looked again with a spark of recognition.

"Jean-Paul?" she questioned.

"Babette!" responded the man who was a few years older than Babette. "It is so good to see you! What are you doing here on Mount Everest?"

Babette introduced Bridget, Barnaby, and Beauregard to Jean-Paul, a friend from Paris. Then she briefly explained their mission on behalf of UNICEF. As they talked, Jean-Paul guided them into the warmth of a nearby tent.

"I had wondered how you were going to spend the summer," grinned Jean-Paul. "I know how you lose your patience with all those tourists who descend on Paris!"

Babette blushed at the thought of a cute guy like Jean-Paul

noticing such things, and redirected the conversation. "What are you doing here in the Himalayas, Jean-Paul?"

"Climbing Mount Everest, of course!" Jean-Paul cried exultantly. "My mountain-climbing club has climbed mountains on several continents, and this summer we wanted to climb the highest mountain in the world. We just got back from the summit yesterday."

"Since we're learning about geography and you seem to know quite a bit about mountains, would you tell us about some of the mountains you have visited?" asked Barnaby, wanting to hear more from this adventurous new acquaintance.

"Why, of course!" Jean-Paul replied with a friendly smile. "Since starting to climb a number of years ago, I have come to respect the demands of the mountains as well as the powers that formed them millions of years ago."

Noting the interest in the questers' faces, Jean-Paul continued, "The earth has an outer covering much like the shell of an egg. This thick shell covering is divided into large connecting pieces, something like a jigsaw puzzle. These pieces making up the earth's shell are called plates. The lines where the plates come in contact with each other are called faults or fault lines. As the earth has evolved over millions of years, these plates have crashed into each other and mountains have formed.

"Many mountains formed when layers of rock making up the earth's surface buckled as the plates collided. The rocks either moved up through the cracks or folded, accordion-like, along the fault lines. The Himalayas were formed by this folding action.

"Some of the mountains I have climbed are the result of volcanic formations created when the friction of rubbing plates and open areas causes melted rock material to push up to the surface. Mount Kilimanjaro, which I climbed two years ago, is an example of a volcanic mountain. These mountains may be domed or cone-shaped, and they continue to release melted rock during periodic eruptions."

"Like Mount St. Helen's in the Cascade Range of North America," interjected Bridget as she remembered a film about volcanoes from school last year.

"Yes, that is a perfect example of an active volcanic mountain," responded Jean-Paul eagerly. "Not all volcanic mountains remain active, thank goodness, just as other mountain ranges differ from each other in various ways. For example, mountains were formed at different times as our earth evolved. The Appalachian Mountains in North America are very old and have been worn down and rounded by wind and water over millions of years. Another North American mountain range, the Rocky Mountains, are much younger. The craggy peaks of the Rockies have not had as many years of exposure to the elements."

"Have you climbed mountains on all the continents?" Barnaby asked as he envisioned some of the peaks of the Andes near Lake Titicaca.

"Not all—yet!" said Jean-Paul with a laugh. "I have many more adventures in the mountains planned. However, I will not be able to climb some of the tallest mountains on earth, because they are under the ocean. The plates crashed together under the oceans, too, forming mountains which rose from their floors."

"That's right!" exclaimed Babette, as she recalled learning that islands are often the result of the ocean-floor formation of mountain ranges or volcanic mountains.

"Our clue to the next cylinder in our mission hints that we will go to 'the top of the world,'" Bridget said as she looked at the piece of paper. "That sounds like we'll have to climb Mount Everest, doesn't it?"

"It would seem so," Jean-Paul replied, suddenly quite serious as he looked at the group. "But mountain climbing is very dangerous, and the air is very thin at this altitude. It will be a very difficult, exhausting task."

Beauregard began to ponder what he was going to have to do in order to rescue Bridget, Barnaby, and Babette from themselves and the situations they were getting into, when his thoughts were interrupted by Babette asking Jean-Paul to teach them some mountain-climbing skills.

The next few days were spent learning the skills the questers would need to climb Mount Everest. Each session had to be quite short since the group was not yet accustomed to the lower level of oxygen at the high altitude. They came to understand what Jean-Paul meant about becoming tired in the thin mountain air.

When they were ready to make the climb to the summit, Barnaby found a few ropes and picks by searching through his bushy hair. "My parents and I needed these when we were studying the rare Pallywocker bird, which nests on cliff faces," he said. "I remember now that my dad stuck these in my hair so they wouldn't get lost."

Jean-Paul, having heard of the treasure trove Barnaby carried around on his head, was still a little surprised at how many large objects could be found there. When he saw that the flow had stopped, however, he went off to get the questers the rest of the equipment they would need for their climb.

✍ QUIZ #12 ✍

Checking Out Mountains

1. Some mountains are formed when plates on the earth's shell crash into each other, buckling and folding along the fault lines. An example is the Himalayas. Other mountains are the result of volcanic formations. What causes volcanic mountains like Mount Kilimanjaro in Africa?

2. What happens when a volcano becomes inactive?

3. Using an atlas, list the highest mountains on every continent. Next list the five highest mountains in the world.

4. In North America, why are the Rocky Mountains taller than the Appalachian Mountains? (See fig. 4, p. 23.)

5. Why can't Jean-Paul climb all the mountains in the world?

6. Look at all of the continent maps (fig. 4, p. 23; fig. 14, p. 48; fig. 21, p. 72; fig. 23, p. 81; fig. 25, p. 93; fig. 31, p. 124; fig. 34, p. 140) and label any mountain ranges you find. For example, the Rocky Mountains in North America and the Andes in South America.

7. How much taller is Mount Everest than Mount McKinley?

8. A mile is 5,280 feet, and one yard equals three feet. How many yards high is Mount Everest?

9. How many miles high is Mount Everest?

10. If you could climb any mountain at the rate of 10 feet per minute, how long would it take to climb Mount McKinley?

     ✻ ✻ ✻ ✻ ✻

"See you back in Paris this fall," Jean-Paul said to Babette as he kissed her on both cheeks. "And good luck, everyone!"

Babette's blushing cheeks warmed her as she set off up Mount Everest with her friends. They left the camp early in the morning in order to reach the summit before dark. Beauregard also cautiously kept an eye on the sky and clouds since he knew that fierce storms could come up quickly on Mount Everest, bringing strong, frigid winds and blinding snow.

The adventurers climbed for hours, using the picks to secure footholds as they inched their way up the trail of ice and snow. Beauregard led the group—being a large cat with sharp claws, he was the most adept at climbing. He was followed by Babette, Bridget and, finally, Barnaby.

As they neared the summit, Babette called to Beauregard, "I'm nearly frozen from the cold, Beauregard. I don't think I can go on. She started to sit down in the snow as Beauregard rushed toward her.

"No! Don't sit down—you've got to keep moving," he said. It's very dangerous for a climber to stop and lose precious time."

"We'll be at the summit very soon now," Beauregard continued, as he used his bulk to brace Babette. "I'll climb with you these last few feet."

Sure enough, it wasn't long before the summit of Mount Everest came into view. Almost immediately, Beauregard saw the sunlight reflecting off something else besides the snow.

"I think that's the cylinder," Beauregard said to Babette, hoping to urge her on. "Let me give you one last boost so you can reach the summit and get it."

With his claws dug firmly into the ice, Beauregard was able to help Babette the last few steps to the summit. A quick glance around and she located the cylinder, which she grabbed although the cold had taken all sensation from her hands.

The four friends celebrated their ascent to the top of the world quickly, sitting on the freezing, wind-swept summit. Beauregard took the clue from the cylinder and read it to the others:

Feeling on top of the world—or just cold? BVM

Clue #11: 45 degrees north latitude and 110 degrees east longitude—The ponies walk on land that is as flat as a line, while the people live in houses as round as circles!

"I wonder what this clue will bring?" Bridget wondered.

"Hopefully the worst is over," said Beauregard as he set the latitude and longitude numbers on the Coordinator. "It can't get more challenging than climbing Mount Everest, can it?"

Bridget, Barnaby, Babette, and Beauregard soon realized that their parkas wouldn't be necessary in their new location. While not extremely hot, the weather was certainly warm enough to encourage them to put their coats back into the pack. All they could see was a flat, treeless expanse and some small, rounded hills on the horizon. The dry soil contained many small stones and was dotted with clumps of short grass.

"That looks like a dust cloud over there," said Bridget as she pointed to their right.

As the dust cloud came closer, however, it became clear that it was generated by a group of ponies galloping across the dry landscape.

"They may be the ponies the clue mentioned," remarked Barnaby as he watched the approaching animals.

"And one of them appears to have a rider," added Babette.

Soon, several of the ponies trotted by the four friends, slowing down only for a passing glance at the strangers. The other ponies followed a few moments later, one of them with a rider. The rider was a girl about Bridget's age with long, dark hair tied back from her round face. She had dark, almond-shaped eyes and a bright smile that she flashed at the newcomers.

"Hello," the girl said as she stopped in front of Bridget, Barnaby, Babette, and Beauregard. "I don't think I've ever met anyone just standing out here before. Where are your ponies?"

Bridget spoke up, "We just sort of arrived here and we don't have ponies. Do you live around here?"

"Yes, well, sort of. I'm staying with my grandmother for a few weeks this summer. My name is Katya," the girl said as she got down from her pony.

Bridget introduced herself and her friends, and briefly explained why they were in the area. Katya invited the travelers to her grandmother's house for lunch, and rounded up ponies for them to ride.

"There's not much here for you to see," Katya began as the group began to move off. "The Gobi Desert area is only sparsely populated, and many of the people move from place to place with their herds."

"You said you were staying with your grandmother for a few weeks," Babette said as her pony trotted along beside Katya's. "Where do you live the rest of the year?"

"With my parents, brothers, and sisters in Siberia," replied the questers' new friend. "The Central Siberian Plateau (fig. 25, p. 93) is north of here. I spend the summers here at my grandmother's because it gets so cold in the far north. In fact, the ground never thaws where I live."

"Never?" said Bridget, shivering at the thought of an area so cold that the ground stayed permanently frozen.

"No," answered Katya. "We live in an area called the **tundra** (fig. 29, p. 109) where the ground is called **permafrost**. This means that the soil is permanently frozen. During the summer months the top few inches of soil may thaw enough to support some vegetation. However, the remaining soil and small rocks are 'cemented' together by frozen ice crystals."

"Your area doesn't get very much precipitation, does it?" asked Barnaby, remembering that very cold air is usually devoid of moisture.

"No, it doesn't," Katya said, turning to Barnaby. "And that's just as well, because the frozen soil will not allow water to penetrate. In summer, when most of the precipitation occurs, the temperature never rises above 50 degrees Fahrenheit. In winter, our average temperature is -40 degrees Fahrenheit."

"Minus forty degrees!" exclaimed Babette. "I can see why the ground is permanently frozen."

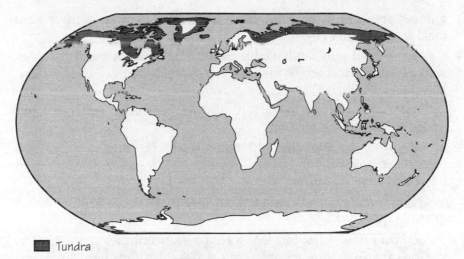

Tundra

Figure 29: Areas of tundra

"And why you like to visit your grandmother in a warmer climate during the summer," added Bridget.

Beauregard was hoping the tundra wasn't on their travel itinerary when the ponies approached a group of tents. The tents, made of material that resembled very heavy felt, looked a little like circus tents except the tops were rounded. There was a small smokestack coming out of the top of each one.

"These are called yurts," Katya informed the group as she observed the interest in their faces. "My grandmother lives in this one over here."

Katya showed the questers how to tie the ponies, and they

entered the tent to be greeted by an elderly woman with a kind face and warm eyes.

"I'm so glad you can have lunch with us," Katya's grandmother said as she welcomed the visitors. "We rarely see new faces around here."

"There was that visitor a few days ago," Katya reminded her grandmother. "Remember?"

"Oh, yes!" recalled the old woman as she bent down to get something from behind a pile of rugs. "A traveler came by and left this."

"A cylinder!" exclaimed Bridget, Barnaby, Babette, and Beauregard.

"So you know what this is?" Katya's grandmother replied. "The visitor said that some people would pass through here soon and would know what to do with this. I suppose it belongs to you then." She handed the cylinder to Babatte and went to prepare lunch for her guests.

"Bridget..." whispered Babette.

"Shhh," Bridget responded. "I don't want to think about it—it's too spooky."

After enjoying lunch with Katya and her grandmother, the questers said their good-byes and walked outside, where they opened the cylinder and read the next clue.

One more Asian visit to go! BVM

Clue #12: 23.5 degrees north latitude and 40 degrees east longitude—Keep on the same latitude, from sea to sea—from one of sand to one of water!

"We're really going to travel this time," observed Babette. "We're at 110 degrees east latitude and I'm setting the Coordinator for 40 degrees east longitude."

"The clue mentioned the sea," reminded Beauregard. "Look on the map to make sure we won't land in water again."

"Don't worry, Beauregard, we'll be on land," Bridget reported after she consulted the guidebook map. "It looks like we're going to the Arabian Peninsula." (See fig. 25, p. 93.)

"Hold on, everybody," Babette said as he pushed the green button.

✍ QUIZ #13 ✍
Permafrost and the Tundra

1. How does the Central Siberian Plain differ in the summer and the winter?

2. At what level of latitude does the tundra begin?

3. Why do you think there are no tundras in the southern hemisphere?

Chapter 8

Deserts: More than Heat and Sand

The glare of seemingly endless sand under the sun's rays was almost as bright as the snow on Mount Everest. The sand went on and on, in rolling dunes, one after another.

"It really does look like a sea of sand—just like the clue said," Babette observed.

"I've been thinking about that clue," Barnaby said after a few minutes. "It mentions keeping on the same latitude, which is now 23.5 degrees north. Didn't we dial that same latitude before?"

"Yes, we did," recalled Babette. "23.5 degrees north latitude was one of the coordinates that took us to the delta in southern Asia where the monsoon rains were occurring."

"The different climates really do occur at the same degree of latitude," Beauregard commented as he looked around the arid landscape for some sign of vegetation.

"This location, 23.5 degrees north latitude, is called the Tropic of Cancer," Babette reported after consulting the guidebook, "and 23.5 degrees south latitude is called the Tropic of Capricorn."

"But what does that mean?" Bridget asked.

"Remember we learned that the tropic zone is the area of earth that receives direct rays from the sun?" Babette reminded her friends. "Well, the Tropic of Cancer is the northern boundary of the tropic zone, and the Tropic of Capricorn is the southern boundary."

"It sure seems like we're getting the sun's direct rays now," Barnaby said, beginning to feel the heat at the base of a sand dune.

"Look over here!" shouted Beauregard from the top of another sand dune. As usual, Beauregard was checking out the area.

Bridget, Babette, and Barnaby scrambled up the dune to see what Beauregard was so excited about.

"It's an oasis," Beauregard announced as he directed the kids' gaze to a point over the sand dune. "They really do need a more savvy companion along," he thought to himself as the others gaped at the pool of water surrounded by palm trees.

"We need to make sure this isn't just a mirage," cautioned Barnaby as that gleam of scientific knowledge entered his eyes. "You know an optical illusion can occur when the warm desert air near the ground bends the light rays from the sky and creates an image of pools of water on the sand."

"I don't think an illusion would include palm trees!" exclaimed Beauregard as he started off in the direction of the oasis, somewhat insulted that Barnaby had questioned the validity of his discovery.

Bridget, Babette, and Barnaby followed Beauregard and the travelers soon arrived at the oasis. They saw tents under the palm trees, and camels tethered a little further off. And the oasis was certainly a busy place—there were people everywhere.

"Hello, there!" called Bridget to a man tending a group of camels.

"Welcome to the oasis, travelers!" he answered with a smile. "Come and rest from your trip across the sands. My name is Abdul and these are my family's tents."

"Do you live here at the oasis?" asked Babette as she looked at the children running around between the tents, interrupting the rest of some goats.

"Oh, no," replied Abdul. "We are Bedouins, a nomadic people who travel the desert. Every oasis is our home. Please be our guests—you must rest from your travels."

Abdul guided the four friends to a nearby tent and offered them cool drinks and pillows to rest on. Bridget, Barnaby, Babette, and Beauregard were once again appreciating the kindness of a stranger on their quest.

"Where are you going, my new friends?" queried Abdul.

"To the sea," Bridget replied, remembering that the clue had indicated that they should travel "from sea to sea."

"And so are we," remarked Abdul. "You and your friends are welcome to join our caravan. There are extra camels, and we will be leaving tomorrow."

"Why, thank you, we'd like that," Beauregard replied, grasping the opportunity to avoid trekking mile after mile on foot through the rolling sand.

The four adventurers pitched in that evening to help the Bedouin family prepare for their departure the next morning. The desert cooled after sunset, so everyone was able to get a good night's rest.

The next day, the friends became acquainted with the art of camel riding. It wasn't as difficult as they expected, despite the humps. Abdul talked to the questers as they traveled, pointing out interesting facts about the desert terrain.

"You sure know a lot about deserts," Barnaby observed.

"I should, since they have always been my home!" laughed Abdul.

Bridget explained to Abdul that they were on a journey to learn more about the earth, including its deserts, and asked him to tell them more.

"I would be honored to share what I know with you," Abdul began. "Most people think of **deserts** as hot, dry places. They are partially correct—all deserts are dry, but only some are hot. The term desert actually refers to a region that receives less than 10 inches of precipitation a year. There are four main types of deserts in the world: subtropical, interior, coastal, and polar."

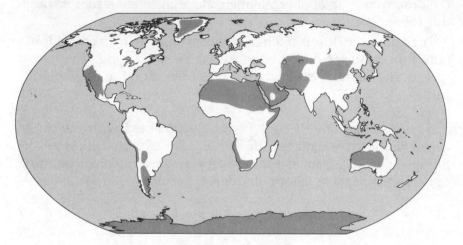

Figure 30: Deserts

"And we are in a subtropical desert here, right?" contributed Beauregard as he took another sip of water from the canteen around his neck. The sun was getting hotter now that it was nearly midday.

"Correct," smiled Abdul as he tossed a head covering to Beauregard to help fend off the heat. "Our Arabian Desert and the Kalahari Desert in Africa are examples of subtropical deserts. However, the Sahara in northern Africa is the most famous subtropical desert. It covers most of the top third of the continent and is the world's largest desert. Sand dunes can reach over 1,000 feet high there, and the fierce sandstorms can blow for hundreds of miles. Sand makes up only approximately 20 percent of the Sahara, however, the rest being covered with rock, gravel, and salt deposits. Day temperatures can soar to over 100 degrees Fahrenheit in a subtropical desert during the day, but may cool down quickly to below 50 degrees Fahrenheit at night."

"I noticed that the temperature became much cooler last night," observed Babette.

"Yes," replied Abdul. "That's because the dry air of the desert doesn't retain heat once the sun sets. When you look at a map, you may notice that subtropical deserts often occur in the western half of a continent or west of a mountain range, and that's because the winds in these areas have often lost their moisture. You will also notice that subtropical deserts tend to occur between 20 and 25 degrees north or south latitude, along the Tropic of Cancer and the Tropic of Capricorn."

"We discussed being on the latitude of the Tropic of Cancer when we arrived," said Bridget, thinking about how a lot of the information they had learned was beginning to fit together now.

"And so you are," Abdul added. "But, as I said, subtropical deserts are only one type of desert," he continued. "In the temperate climate zones of the hemispheres' middle latitudes, you will find interior deserts. Because winds coming from the oceans usually lose their moisture upon reaching land, these deserts are found toward the middle of continents. An interior desert has hot summers and very cold winters. Examples of this kind of desert can be found in South America, the United States, and Asia."

"Actually, we were in the Gobi Desert recently," said Barnaby, realizing how well Bartholomew Van Morrow had planned their amazing journey.

"I understand the winters there are bitterly cold," noted Abdul. He had no desire to experience such a winter, being so accustomed to the heat of his homeland.

"Coastal deserts are usually found in the southern hemisphere where cold ocean currents deprive some coastal areas of moisture," Abdul continued. "Because ocean storms are cooled as they pass over the currents, moisture is released from the air before it reaches land. The Namib Desert in southwest Africa is a coastal desert. The Namib gleans moisture from the thick fog caused by the cool ocean winds meeting the warmer air of the land, but it receives very little precipitation. The driest desert on earth, the Atacama Desert in South America, is also a coastal desert. This desert is made particularly dry because the high Andes Mountains stop storms from bringing in moisture from the east. It has been reported that areas of the Atacama Desert went without rain for 400 years—from 1570 until 1971! Since modern rain detectors have been in use, some areas of this desert haven't recorded any precipitation."

The thought of such a dry place made Beauregard take another swig from his canteen. The head covering Abdul had given him was helping to ward off the heat, but he found himself longing for the trade winds of Montego Bay.

"Have you been to any polar regions on your travels?" inquired Abdul.

"Yes," replied Bridget. "We stopped in at Antarctica."

"Then you were in a desert!" exclaimed Abdul. "Polar deserts, the last major type of desert, are found over Antarctica and parts of Greenland. The air in these regions is too cold to retain moisture, and the annual precipitation of snow is equivalent to two inches of rainfall. The snow that falls on these polar deserts never melts, it simply adds to the snow that formed the ice cap hundreds of years ago."

"An ice cap!" thought Babette. "How refreshing that sounds."

As the sun began to set and the air cooled down, the caravan reached another oasis. The explorers helped Abdul's family set up the tents, freshened up, and spent some time looking at a map with Abdul.

"We should be at the Red Sea by tomorrow," Abdul told them as he pointed to their location on the map. "I wish you a restful night. I will see you in the morning."

✍ QUIZ #14 ✍
Checking Out Deserts and Seas

1. What is the significance of the Tropic of Cancer and the Tropic of Capricorn? In other words, what do the imaginary lines found at 23.5 degrees north and south of these areas indicate?

2. There are four types of deserts in the world: subtropical, interior, coastal, and polar (see fig. 30, p. 116). Use the information in this chapter to explain the differences between the four types of deserts.

3. Define the term sea. Find the largest sea in the world and the deepest sea in the world.

4. The Dead Sea is the saltiest body of water on earth. Why do you think this is?

5. Using all the continental maps (fig. 4, p. 23; fig. 14, p. 48; fig. 21, p. 72; fig. 23, p. 81; fig. 25, p.93; fig. 31, p. 124; fig. 34, p.140), list as many seas as you can find.

✍ EXERCISE #11 ✍
Library Activity

1. Go to the library and research how far the earth tilts on its axis toward the sun during the longest and shortest days in the northern hemisphere.

2. Why do daytime and nighttime temperatures in the Sahara Desert in northern Africa differ so dramatically?

✎ ✎ ✎ ✎ ✎

After Abdul left, the travelers looked over the map and guidebook a few more minutes to learn more about their destination.

"It says in the guidebook that a **sea** is a small body of water that lies along the margins of an ocean," read Bridget.

"Like the Mediterranean Sea to the south of France," noted Babette. "It is very beautiful there."

"And we're going to the Red Sea," Barnaby said as he looked at the map, "which separates the Arabian Peninsula from the continent of Africa."

"It says here that the Red Sea is the saltiest body of water on earth," Bridget said, closing the guidebook." There are so many interesting facts about the places we're visiting."

Bridget, Barnaby, Babette, and Beauregard continued with the caravan the next day until they reached the Red Sea. There they bade Abdul and his family good-bye with thanks for their great hospitality.

As they neared the shore of the sea, the questers thought back to the last clue.

"Does anyone know if our journey to the Red Sea has kept

us on the same latitude?" asked Barnaby, remembering that the clue stressed the Tropic of Cancer and traveling from the sea of sand to the sea of water.

"I'm not sure," Babette responded, a little worried. "Do you think we are off course?"

"That survey team down there might help us out," suggested Beauregard as he looked down the shoreline to a group of surveyors.

"My dad's friend showed me how to use surveying equipment once," remarked Barnaby as he headed off down the shore toward the survey team.

Barnaby was peering through one of the pieces of equipment when Bridget, Babette, and Beauregard arrived. Beauregard, being curious by nature, also wanted to look through the lens of the equipment. He was feeling a little irked with Barnaby. "I was the one who spotted it in the first place," he grumbled to himself as he looked around for another vacant piece of equipment. He spotted a stack of cases marked "Survey Instruments" and walked over in the hope of finding one.

Babette, who had been looking out over the calm sea, glanced in Beauregard's direction just in time to see his eyes widen with surprise.

"What is it, Beauregard?" she called.

All Beauregard could do was point excitedly—no sound seemed capable of coming out of his open mouth. Babette and Bridget hurried over to their friend to see what the matter was. When they reached him, Beauregard was pointing into an instrument case he had opened.

"It's another cylinder!" cried Babette with surprise. "Oh, Beauregard, now I see why you are speechless. Who would have thought to look in here?"

"Who indeed," thought Bridget as she wondered how their movements could have been predicted so well by Mr. Van Morrow. "Something's going on, but I don't know what—yet."

Barnaby, who seemed to have entered some sort of trance in front of the surveying instrument, missed the discovery of the cylinder. Finally, however, he came to and reported to the others that they were still at 23.5 degrees north latitude.

"Where are we going next?" he asked as he noticed Babette pulling the next clue out of the cylinder.

Ready for continent number 6? BVM

Clue #13: 5 degrees south latitude and 35 degrees east longitude—Participate in a wildlife adventure in the shadows of Mount Kilimanjaro!

"Mount Kilimanjaro!" exclaimed Bridget. "That means we're headed to Africa."

"And meeting wildlife," thought Beauregard as he wondered if any of his distant African relatives would display any feline friendliness to their South Carolina cousin.

Chapter 9
Africa: Savannas and Grasslands

On their arrival in Africa, Beauregard quickly scanned the area for any wildlife, related or otherwise. All he could see, however, was an expanse of flat, grass-covered land scattered with a few low trees, and some mountains on the horizon.

"Whew!" he thought to himself. "At least no lions have dropped by to say hello—or any other menacing creatures."

Meanwhile, Bridget had spotted some buildings surrounded by a tall fence in the direction of the mountains. "Let's walk toward those buildings," she suggested. "It may be a farm or something, and we can find out more about our location."

"I've already looked up our coordinates in the guidebook," said Barnaby as the four friends walked along a beaten-down strip of grass, perhaps a road, leading to the buildings. "It indicates that we are on the Serengeti Plain, an area between Lake Victoria to the west and Mount Kilimanjaro to the east."

"Mount Kilimanjaro," remarked Babette, looking toward the mountain range. "That is the highest mountain in Africa."

"And it was formed by volcanic action," Bridget added.

"Oh, yes," smiled Babette as she thought back to their visit to Mount Everest. "That is the mountain Jean-Paul climbed two years ago."

"The guidebook says that a plain is a broad, flat expanse of land," Barnaby reported, leafing through the guidebook as he walked.

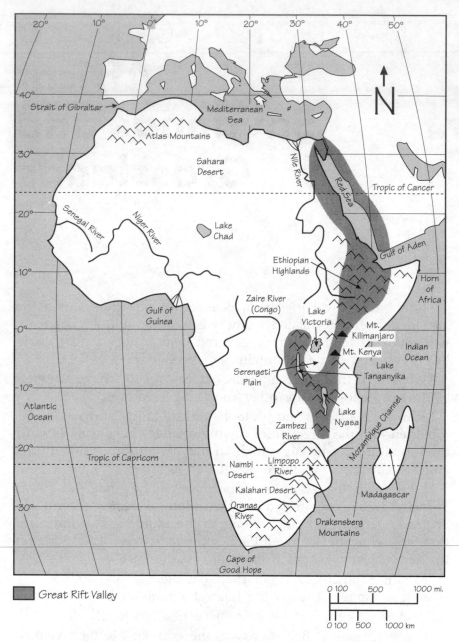

Figure 31: Africa

"That's certainly what we have here," observed Beauregard as he continued to scan the terrain, having seen what appeared to be several giraffes standing by a tree in the distance.

Bridget, Barnaby, Babette, and Beauregard reached the tall fence enclosing the buildings. Beside the open gate a sign read: "Serengeti Wildlife Park—Outpost #4." The questers entered to find three buildings, with a few trees standing between them. No people were to be seen, but the four friends also noticed some large cages at the back of one of the buildings.

"Hello, there!" came a voice out of the stillness, causing the adventurers to jump. Looking over their shoulders, they saw a man emerge from one of the buildings.

"Sorry," the man said as he approached the visitors. "I didn't mean to startle you. I'm Joseph Thuku, the veterinarian for this part of the wildlife park."

Bridget, Barnaby, Babette, and Beauregard shook Dr. Thuku's hand as they introduced themselves.

"I don't think I've ever had visitors arrive on foot before," observed Dr. Thuku. "Walking across the wildlife park can be rather dangerous, you know."

"Our transportation let us off near here," Bridget answered vaguely. She knew the Coordinator would require a long explanation. "We are traveling on a mission for the United Nations this summer, visiting different parts of the world."

"You've certainly come to an interesting part here," Dr. Thuku said, looking proudly at the surrounding landscape. "The park is a refuge for many types of African wildlife; we strive to protect all of the species. In fact, a wounded zebra wandered up here early this morning, and I was checking on him when you arrived. Would you like to see some of the animals I've been treating?"

"Oh yes!" exclaimed Barnaby as the possibility of gaining new scientific knowledge presented itself. "Where are they?"

"Over here," Dr. Thuku indicated as he walked toward the building with the large cages at the back.

The veterinarian showed the questers lions, zebras, and other animals that had wandered into the outpost or had been brought there sick or injured. A gazelle with a bandaged leg captured Babette's heart with its soft, lustrous eyes. "The animals are so beautiful," she commented to Dr. Thuku. "You must enjoy working with them."

"Yes, I do," he replied. "It's very rewarding to see the animals get better and return to the park."

"Do you have any monkeys here?" inquired Bridget, whose favorite part of the Bronx Zoo was the monkey area.

"Not in this area," Dr. Thuku replied. "Monkeys live in the forested lands northwest of here. This area is a savanna where animals such as lions, elephants, giraffes, zebras, and gazelles live."

"Savanna?" queried Bridget.

"Yes," said Dr. Thuku. "**Savannas** are areas in tropical or subtropical zones of the world that border or surround rain forests. Savannas have wet and dry seasons due to the seasonal drift of the doldrums."

"That is the low-pressure area near the equator, isn't it?" Babette recalled.

"You're exactly right!" remarked Dr. Thuku, smiling at his guests. "Rainfall may total 5 to 10 inches a month during the wet season. The rain is brought by the equatorial low-pressure areas. So, the further away from the equator a savanna is located, the less precipitation it has during the wet season."

"What is the dry season like?" wondered Bridget.

"Months may pass without precipitation in the dry season," the veterinarian replied, looking up at the cloudless sky. "However, the wet season provides enough rainfall to support the scattered trees and thick grass of the savanna. One-third of Africa is savanna area that surrounds the rain forest in the central part of the continent (see fig. 32, opposite). Savannas may go by a different name in South America: In Venezuela they are called *llanos*, while in Brazil they are called *campos*."

"When my mother and I drove across the United States several years ago, I saw miles of grassland," Bridget stated. "Was that a savanna?"

"No," Dr. Thuku said, shaking his head. "That was a **steppe**— sometimes called **grassland**. Steppes are found in subtropical and temperate regions, bordering interior deserts. They are flat, semi-arid areas which have sparse vegetation in the subtropics but support more abundant plant life in the middle latitudes. Their temperatures fall at night, and grasslands located far from the equator experience very cold winters."

"I don't remember anyone calling the area we went through a steppe or a grassland," Bridget recalled.

Dr. Thuku smiled, "It's the 'name game' again! In South America, grasslands are called **pampas**, while in North America they are called **prairies**. Steppes or grasslands can be found in the western United States and Canada, South America, south-central Asia, south of the Sahara Desert in Africa, and bordering the Western Australian desert."

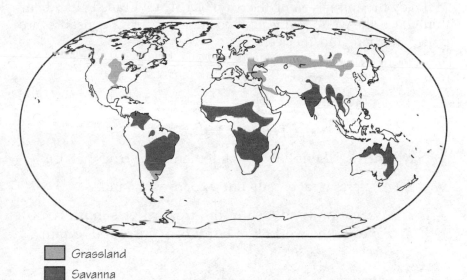

Grassland
Savanna

Figure 32: Savanna and grassland areas

Suddenly, a sharp ringing sound pierced the calm surroundings.

"That's the telephone," explained Dr. Thuku. "It has a very loud ring so I can hear it when I'm outside. Excuse me while I answer it."

Returning after a few minutes, Dr. Thuku said, "That was Outpost #2. They're out of a type of medicine we use for the animals and they need to borrow some. I have to stay here with the zebra that came in this morning, so I can't go. I wonder if I could persuade you to take one of the jeeps and deliver it for me?"

"We would love to do an errand for you," volunteered Babette, thinking how exciting a ride through the wildlife park would be.

"Great!" replied Dr. Thuku with a grateful grin. "I'll draw a map for you. You'll travel along a road much like the one that comes into this outpost. I didn't catch the name of the person who called from Outpost #2—must be a new veterinarian."

Ten minutes later, Beauregard was sitting at the wheel of the jeep. He'd been on expeditions like this before, although none in a place where he might be seen at the wheel of a jeep by one of his relatives prowling around at the side of the road. He studied the map Dr. Thuku had given him and, as soon as the box containing the medicine and the kids were aboard, he took off down the road.

"Enjoy the animals along the way!" Dr. Thuku called after them, thinking of the weird, feline juxtaposition occurring as Beauregard pulled his tail into the jeep.

✍ QUIZ #15 ✍
True or False

Say whether the following statements are true or false.

1. A plain is a broad, flat expanse of land.

2. A savanna is an area in the tropical or subtropical zones of the world that borders or surrounds a rain forest.

3. Savannas have wet and dry seasons due to the seasonal drift of the doldrums.

4. Rainfall may total 5 to 10 inches per month during the wet season.

5. The rain is brought by equatorial high-pressure areas.

6. The further away from the equator a savanna is located, the more precipitation or rainfall it has during the wet season.

7. Months may pass without rain during the dry season, but the wet season provides enough rainfall to support the scattered trees and thick grass of a savanna.

8. One-third of Africa consists of savanna, which surrounds the rain forest in the middle of the continent.

9. Beauregard's cousin, the lion, lives in a savanna known as the Serengeti Plains in Africa.

10. Savannas may go by different names. In South America, they are called *llanos* in Venezuela and *campos* in Brazil.

11. A steppe is sometimes called a grassland. It is found in either subtropical or temperate regions bordering interior deserts.

12. Steppes have sparse vegetation in the subtropics, but support more abundant plant life in the middle latitudes.

13. When a grassland is located near the equator, the winters can be very cold.

14. In South America, grasslands are called prairies.

15. In North America, grasslands are called pampas.

✏ ✏ ✏ ✏ ✏

The questers saw many animals on their way to Outpost #2, and some of them did indeed appear to squint at the driver of the jeep. At one point a huge lion roared loudly toward them, making Beauregard even more paranoid. "I'm so glad to be part of a well-established family with a home in South Carolina," he told himself. "Imagine being stuck out here—stifling hot during one part of the year and soaking wet during the other. It would play havoc with my fur, not to mention my social life!"

As the jeep approached Outpost #2, the questers spotted a piece of paper attached to a large mailbox at the gate.

"That might be a note for us about the medicine," Barnaby suggested as Beauregard slowed the jeep in front of the box.

Babette reached out and grabbed the piece of paper. "Dear Courier: Had to leave for a while—please leave the medicine in the box. Thank you, Outpost #2 Veterinarian."

Barnaby hopped out of the jeep with the medicine and pulled open the lid of the mailbox. "There's a cylinder in here!" he shouted in surprise, lifting the metallic tube from the mailbox.

Bridget and Babette looked at each other, wondering who had really called Dr. Thuku at the outpost. Barnaby, being caught up in loftier ideas, hadn't seemed to notice these weird connections. He placed the medicine in the mailbox and opened the cylinder.

Keep up the good work! BVM

Clue #14: 30 degrees north latitude and 31 degrees east longitude—Float down the Nile River like Cleopatra, but stop to enjoy the pyramids and the Great Sphinx.

"Floating down the Nile sounds like it might have possibilities," thought Beauregard as he envisioned floating on a tent-covered barge, eating luscious fruit and being cooled by fan-bearing attendants. He knew that, at least in ancient times, cats were considered sacred in this area.

"Another desert?" said Babette as she shifted her feet in the hot mixture of sand and gravel at the questers' new destination.

"I thought we were supposed to float down the Nile," said Bridget.

"That'll have to come later, I guess," said Barnaby.

Beauregard said nothing.

"I think I see some water beyond those tents over there," Bridget observed, perking up a little. "Let's head in that direction."

The adventurers arrived at the group of tents a while later. These tents weren't like those of the Bedouin family in the Arabian Desert—they were more modern and the camp was occupied by people wearing khaki shorts and shirts rather than flowing robes.

Beauregard's mouth dropped open with surprise as he stared at one of the passing camp occupants. "Ludwig?" he said as the man returned his look of recognition.

"Why, Beauregard, my old friend!" the man cried as he came over to the questers. "I haven't seen you since that dig in Mexico several years ago. Are you and your friends planning to join our expedition here?"

Beauregard introduced his old friend Ludwig to Bridget, Barnaby, and Babette and explained that they were just passing through on a mission for the United Nations. Ludwig, Beauregard told his friends, was an anthropologist who accompanied other scientists on archeological digs all over the world.

"You just arrived here, eh?" noted Ludwig. "Where did you travel from?"

"We were on the Serengeti Plain," cried Barnaby, hopping around excitedly. He'd hardly expected to meet a famous scientist like Ludwig.

"Near the southern part of the Rift Valley then," commented Ludwig.

"Rift Valley?" questioned Bridget.

"Yes," replied Ludwig. "This expedition is headed for part of the Great Rift Valley several hundred miles south of here."

"I don't think we've ever heard about the Great Rift Valley," Babette told Ludwig as the four friends were ushered into his tent for some cool lemonade.

"Well then," responded Ludwig with enthusiasm, "I'll tell you about it!"

Bridget, Babette, and Beauregard settled down with their cool drinks. Barnaby was still hopping around, and the others had to grab hold of him and force him to sit down, whereupon he began to stare at Ludwig in awe. Ludwig, being modest, pretended not to notice Barnaby's mouth hanging open as he began. "You may know that the plates that cover the earth have moved over millions of years and have changed the shape of the land. As two plates move away from each other at a fault line, land between the separating plates can sink, creating a long, narrow valley, called a **rift valley**. The Great Rift Valley of East Africa stretches 3,000 miles, starting at the top of the Arabian Peninsula and continuing southward."

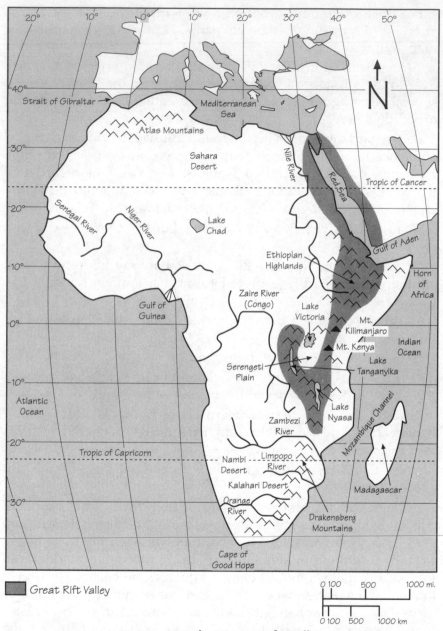

Figure 33: The Great Rift Valley

Beauregard clamped Barnaby's mouth shut as the group gathered around a map of the area. Ludwig continued, "The shift in the earth's plates that resulted in the Great Rift Valley also created the Red Sea and Gulf of Aden. And in an area 30 to 40 miles wide, fossil evidence of early human life has been discovered. That's the reason for this expedition. Besides creating a valley, the shifting of the plates' position also created some long, deep lakes and volcanic mountains."

"Like Mount Kilimanjaro?" Babette asked.

"Correct," Ludwig answered, "and Mount Kenya, too."

"When did the plates stop moving?" Barnaby inquired, finally seeming more normal.

"They haven't stopped yet," said Ludwig as he smiled at Barnaby. "But the plates move so slowly that a change won't be noticed for thousands of years."

"What do you think you will find on your expedition to the Great Rift Valley?" Bridget queried, thinking of the many exciting possibilities.

"We have no idea!" laughed Ludwig. "We'll just explore and see what we can learn."

"That's sort of what we're doing on our travels," noted Bridget. "We learn something everywhere we go."

"Where are you going now?" asked Ludwig, thinking it was a shame that Beauregard and his friends couldn't join the expedition.

"We're supposed to go up the Nile," replied Beauregard as images of fruit, slowly going rotten, crossed his mind.

"On foot?" Ludwig exclaimed, remembering that his old friend and the kids had walked into the camp.

"We hope to float up the Nile...," Beauregard responded wistfully, realizing that his earlier vision was not likely to match the reality.

"Take one of our rafts, Beauregard," offered Ludwig. "We have a few extra, and I can always spare one for an old friend. I can also give you a few supplies. I'll have someone bring you some dried fruit, bread, and other bits and pieces."

The adventurers thanked Ludwig for his kindness as they pushed the raft off the banks of the Nile.

"Well, you never know when we'll meet again," Ludwig told Beauregard as they shook hands and patted each other on the back. "Enjoy yourselves everyone!"

Some Interesting Facts...

- You learned earlier that the earth's crust is made up of plates that connect along fault lines. When these plates crash they may form high mountains, but when they move away from each other the land between them may sink. This latter action may create a long, narrow valley called a rift valley.

- The Great Rift Valley in East Africa stretches 3,000 miles, starting at the top of the Arabian Peninsula and continuing southward.

- The Red Sea and Gulf of Aden were both caused by plates in the earth's crust moving away from each other.

- Fossils found by archeologists provide evidence of early human life.

- Plates are continuing to move, but so slowly that any changes will not be noticed for thousands of years.

✎ ✎ ✎ ✎ ✎

Several hours passed as Bridget, Barnaby, Babette, and Beauregard drifted down the Nile, idly watching the landscape pass slowly by.

"Can you imagine how long it would take to travel the 4,150 miles of the Nile?" Babette commented as she thumbed through the guidebook to pass the time. "The book says that the Nile begins with the White Nile River in Lake Victoria."

"That's near the Serengeti Plain we visited earlier," recalled Barnaby, his interest sparked.

"And it's the largest lake in Africa," Babette added. "The White Nile, which has pale green water, merges with the Blue Nile in Northern Africa to form the Nile River."

"Does the guidebook say if the pyramids and the Great Sphinx are near the river?" asked Bridget as she thought about their clue for the area.

"I think so," Babette said as she turned back to the guidebook.

"No need to look it up," called Beauregard. "There they are over there!"

Babette, Barnaby, and Bridget looked in the direction Beauregard was pointing and saw the huge, pointed structures on the upriver shore. Located close by was the Great Sphinx.

As the raft neared the pyramids, the travelers marveled at their size and at the skill required to construct them.

"And just think, those people had no trucks, no cranes, nothing like that to help them," said Barnaby, awestruck for the second time that day.

The explorers maneuvered the raft toward the river bank and disembarked to take a closer look.

A large group of tourists arrived shortly after Bridget, Barnaby, Babette, and Beauregard reached the first pyramid.

"Let's go over to the Great Sphinx and come back here when they are gone," Babette said, annoyed that they could no longer observe the pyramids in peace.

The questers headed off toward the Great Sphinx.

Arriving at the feet of the Great Sphinx, Bridget struck an amazing, highbrow sort of pose saying, "I am Cleopatra, Queen of the Nile, and you will all do my bidding!"

"Well, Cleopatra better be careful or she'll trip over those rocks," Barnaby replied flatly.

"Oh, Barnaby! You have no imagination!" scolded Bridget as she stepped carefully around the feet of the Great Sphinx. She failed to see a small pile of stones, however, and the next moment she was sprawling on the ground.

"Bridget! Are you hurt?" cried Babette, running over to her friend.

"I'm okay," Bridget replied curtly, scowling in Barnaby's direction. "Hey, wait a minute! There's something under these stones!" Bridget reached down into the pile of stones and, smugly, pulled out a metallic tube.

"The cylinder!" Babette exclaimed. "Good work, Queen of the Nile!"

As Bridget dusted herself off, the others crowded around to read the next clue.

Bravo! On to the last continent! BVM

Clue #15: 47 degrees north latitude and 47 degrees east longitude—The Volga ends in a great depression into a sea that is not a sea!

"What a strange-sounding clue!" remarked Barnaby. "A sea that isn't a sea?"

"We'll have to give this one some more thought when we get there," Bridget said as she pulled the Coordinator out of the backpack.

Babette spoke up, "Hold it! I want to set the Coordinator this time!"

"Okay, okay," sighed Bridget as she handed the machine to Babette. "Let's get going!"

Babette set the dials and the questers left the scene in a flash, leaving the tourists gaping in astonishment. Egypt really was a magic place.

✍ EXERCISE #12 ✍
Cleopatra's Nile

1. Using the map of Africa on page 124 locate Lake Victoria, then trace the 4,150 miles of the longest river in the world to its end. Where does it end?

2. The pyramids were built by ancient people and look like, well, like pyramids—that is, three-dimensional, triangular, geometric shapes. Read more about the Egyptian pyramids in a history text or reference book. What was their purpose?

3. Read about Cleopatra and her role in the early civilization along the Nile.

4. Draw by hand a map of Africa, which happens to look like a large T-bone steak. Label all of the major areas discussed in this chapter. Then draw a line through all the cities the questers would have visited to reach their destination if they had not had the Coordinator. Mark each city on your map.

Chapter 10
Europe: Peninsulas and Fjords

Their latest clue landed the questers near another large river, not in it. They had forgotten to check the coordinates before setting the Coordinator and zooming off to their next destination.

Babette quickly pulled the guidebook out of the backpack before anybody caught on. "We are in Eastern Europe along the southern end of the Volga River," she announced, pointing at a map in the book.

"How do you know we're in Europe?" Bridget questioned. "Europe and Asia seem to run together."

"See the Ural Mountains?" Babette answered, pointing to a mountain range on the map. "The Ural Mountains are the dividing point of Eastern Europe and Asia. We are to the west, or on the European side, of the Ural Mountains. Also, the Volga River is the largest river in Eastern Europe."

"We're not that far from the Caspian Sea," noted Barnaby. "Is that the sea that isn't a sea?"

"That's right!" exclaimed Bridget as she read the guidebook over Babette's shoulder. "It's actually the largest lake in the world and not a sea at all. Remember learning that a sea was a body of water on the margin of an ocean? Well, look at the map—the Caspian Sea is surrounded by land."

"That's right," Barnaby agreed as he noted that the Caspian Sea was encircled by land.

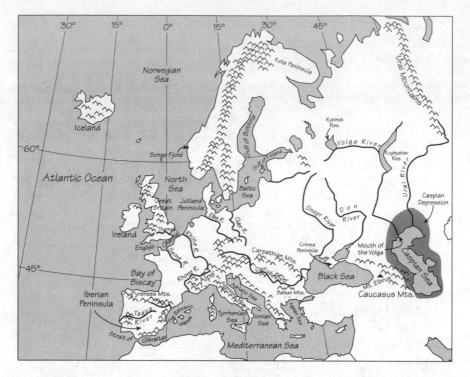

Figure 34: Europe

"It also says here that it is a salt water lake," added Bridget.

"That means it doesn't have an **outlet**. Rivers may flow into it, but nothing flows out," Babette said.

"We *are* remembering something on this trek, aren't we?" Bridget grinned with a sense of accomplishment.

Beauregard had taken the guidebook from Babette; he cleared his throat to get the attention of the others. "And I've found the answer to the remaining mystery of our clue," he began with just a smidgen of self-satisfaction. "The Caspian Depression borders the Caspian Sea. The area of the depression below sea level is the Caspian Sea. In fact, at one point the Caspian Sea is 90 feet below sea level."

"But before we talked about sea level in reference to altitude and high places," said Babette, looking puzzled.

"Sea level is the average height of the world's oceans," Barnaby said slowly as he applied scientific reasoning to the situation. "So the term 'below sea level' must be like altitude in reverse!"

"Now we have all the essential pieces of the clue figured out," Bridget summarized. "And it sounds like we need to follow the Volga River to the Caspian Sea."

Suddenly, the roar of an airplane sent the four questers sprawling to the ground. When they lifted their heads, they saw a small plane swoop overhead and land at a nearby airstrip.

"That plane sounded like it was right on top of us!" exclaimed Babette.

"It almost was!" responded Bridget. "But that gives me an idea about how we could get to the Caspian Sea pretty quickly. I mean, I keep worrying that we'll get delayed somewhere and not find the treasure before the deadline..."

"Do you think we might be able to take a flight down to the Caspian Sea?" asked Barnaby, following Bridget's drift.

"We can always go over to the airstrip and check—you never know what we might find," said Bridget optimistically as she began walking in the direction of the airstrip.

The others joined Bridget, and the questers were soon approaching the main building at the airstrip. A cardboard sign attached to a stake in the grass near the door announced "Caspian Sea Adventure—Departing 2 p.m."

"See!" exclaimed Bridget triumphantly. "I thought we might get lucky! Barnaby, what time is it?"

Barnaby looked at his watch. "One-thirty," he replied. "Let's go in and see if we can still make it."

The four friends entered the building and spotted a group of about twenty people talking and gesturing excitedly.

"Well, that's obviously where we're headed," Bridget stated.

The four questers went over to the group.

"Are you going on the Caspian Sea Adventure?" Babette asked a middle-aged woman.

"Yes, and I'm so excited!" the woman responded with a broad grin. "I've been looking forward to this for months!"

"This trip must be really something," Barnaby whispered to his companions. "The whole group is really hyped up."

"Yeah, they sure are," Bridget agreed. "Why don't we just blend in with them and see if we can get on the plane?"

"I am sure that is possible," Babette replied, nodding her head in the direction of their feline friend.

Beauregard was already being cooed and fussed over by an elderly couple. The woman was exclaiming how cute he was, as the man petted his head and scratched behind his ears. Beauregard wore a look of ultimate, if slightly smug, satisfaction. He caught sight of Bridget and Babette staring at him, and quickly looked away.

The happy group started to move off toward the plane, the kids mingling with the rest of the group and Beauregard walking along between the elderly couple as their special guest.

"You're so charming!" the woman cried.

Bridget rolled her eyes. "I don't believe that cat," she said.

A few minutes later, the entire group was seated in the plane as it sped down the airstrip.

"Off we go!" whispered Barnaby to the others. "So far, so good!"

"I have never flown in an airplane like this," Babette remarked as she looked around the cabin. There were no seats along the sides, no flight attendants or preflight instructions, or even seatbelts. The cabin was quite bare, except for the passengers' benches and a ragged curtain pulled halfway across the entrance to the cockpit. What seemed to be a rather loose door near the front clattered as the plane roared higher into the sky.

"Must be one of those no-frills flights," Barnaby said as a man started handing out small backpacks and helmets to everybody.

"Maybe this is going to be some sort of fly-and-camp trip," suggested Beauregard, leaning across to his friends.

When the man reached the questers, he handed them each a pack and helmet.

"What are these for?" queried Babette.

"For jumping, of course!" said the man with a laugh, as though Babette had made a joke. "We'll be over the jump site soon, and you need to be ready to go!"

"JJJJump?" Bridget exclaimed, barely able to get the word out of her mouth.

"Sure!" the man responded, still smiling happily. "The summer jump to the shore of the Caspian Sea is the highlight of the season. My club looks forward to this all year!"

As the man continued handing out the bundles—now identified

as parachute packs, and helmets to the remaining passengers, the four friends sat in stunned silence. Barnaby's hair stood on end, attaining new heights, and the kitty in the next seat began to quiver uncontrollably. His elderly friends put a little blanket around him, thinking he must be cold.

Eventually, Barnaby leaned over to Bridget and hissed, "We might get lucky. Isn't that what you said?"

"I suddenly do not feel very lucky, Bridget!" Babette chimed in from the other side.

"How was I supposed to know this was a skydiving trip?" Bridget responded defensively. "Who knows, we might like it."

"If we survive," said Barnaby.

"Come on, you two!" Bridget exclaimed. "Where's your spirit, your sense of adventure? Look at Beauregard—he's not whining. He's taking this new development like a real trooper!"

Actually, Beauregard was now frozen with fear. His face, sticking out of the pale blue blanket, was totally still and expressionless. Even his eyes seemed to have glazed over.

"Doesn't anyone know that cats can't stand heights?" Beauregard thought feebly to himself. "I should never have underestimated the ability of these three to get into trouble, and take me with them!"

The man who handed out the equipment returned and, after flicking away Beauregard's blanket, helped the questers to put on their packs and helmets. He showed them both the regular parachute release string and the emergency one.

After helping Beauregard with his pack, the man gave his shoulder a friendly pat, saying, "I know you're concentrating on the jump, pal...but you've got to loosen up a little bit, too!"

"For the first time in a long while, Beauregard thought he could have scratched a human being. "Loosen up indeed!" he pouted as the side door was opened and the occupants began lining up to jump. "I'll loosen up when my four paws are safely back on the ground—if I live that long!"

In line for the door, Beauregard displayed his best Southern manners as he gracefully motioned each person to step ahead of him in the line. The kids were also proving extremely courteous. Soon, Bridget, Barnaby, Babette, and Beauregard were the only passengers left on the plane except for the man who had handed out the equipment. Being the leader of the adventure, the man was holding the door open as each person jumped out.

When Bridget came up to the door, she swallowed hard a few times, closed her eyes, and stepped out, yelling, "Geronimo!"

Not to be outdone by Bridget, Barnaby and Babette also jumped, although they didn't feel the need to shout "Geronimo." Beauregard stopped at the open door and looked down at the shore of the Caspian Sea, far, far below. In response to the view before him, his four paws locked onto the sides of the open door, his claws extended for extra hold.

"I keep telling you, pal...you're concentrating too much!" laughed the man at the door as he gave Beauregard a hearty slap on the back. The slap was just hearty enough to dislodge Beauregard from his locked position and send him tumbling out of the plane.

Sheer survival reflex must have made Beauregard pull the string to release his parachute, and he was soon floating near Bridget, Barnaby, and Babette toward the shore of the Caspian Sea.

Arriving safely on the ground, ~~u~~ other with a mixture of relief and excitem~~...~~ looked at each on the ground beside his parachute, appear~~...~~ard, slumped

"Hey Beauregard! We survived!" said Barn~~...~~ ~~...~~e in shock.

"And in one piece, too," Babette cried, helping ~~t~~ ~~...~~ng. cat to his feet.

black

✍ QUIZ #16 ✍
Time to Review

1. The Ural Mountains are the dividing point of Eastern Europe and Asia. Why is this a logical dividing point?

2. The Volga River is the largest river in Eastern Europe. How does it compare to rivers in North America and South America with respect to length?

3. The Caspian Depression borders the Caspian Sea. This area is below sea level, as is the Caspian Sea. In fact, at its deepest point, the Caspian Sea is 90 feet below sea level. How many yards is 90 feet? A football field is 100 yards long. How does this compare?

4. Sea level is the average height of the world's oceans. Is this reasonable?

5. The term "below sea level" is like altitude in reverse. Explain why this is a realistic statement.

✎ ✎ ✎ ✎ ✎

Beauregard, eager to finish up this latest adventure, pulled at the shoulder straps of his parachute. "Let's get moving now that we're finally here," he remarked nonchalantly, in an effort to dispel any notion that he might have been terrified at having to leap out of an airplane.

Bridget, Barnaby, and Babette had soon removed their harnesses and were rolling the parachutes into a bundle when they noticed Beauregard fiddling with his pack.

"I can't seem to get this off," Beauregard said when he realized "I can't seem others were already free of their packs. "Look at the back his pack, will you? It feels like there's something heavy rolled on there."

Babette came over to assist Beauregard as he turned around for her to inspect his pack. Her eyes widened as she felt inside the pack in an effort to remove the object.

"Beauregard!" Babette whispered with excitement. "It feels like a cylinder!"

"What?" Barnaby and Bridget cried, running over to assist Babette.

With a little tugging and a lot of squirming, the pack was soon off and Babette was holding a cylinder.

"How do you suppose a cylinder got in the parachute pack?" asked Barnaby.

"I'm not sure," Bridget answered, glancing at Babette. "Babette and I have been feeling like we're being shadowed or something on this trip. Have you and Beauregard sensed it?"

"Now that I think about it, things have seemed to turn up just when we needed them," Beauregard said, stroking his chin.

"But, who?" asked Barnaby. "Bartholomew Van Morrow is dead, right?"

"I'm beginning to think anything is possible," sighed Bridget as she pulled the next clue out of the cylinder.

I hope you're enjoying your adventure! BVM

Clue #16: 61 degrees north latitude and 6 degrees east longitude—High mountains and inlet waterways. Everyone ready for another cruise?

"Cruise!" thought Beauregard as he remembered the brief but entirely pleasurable stop at Montego Bay. "Things are looking up again!"

This time, Bridget, Barnaby, Babette, and Beauregard landed on the deck of a ship. It was much smaller than the cruise ship at Montego Bay, and it was sailing down a waterway flanked by tall mountains.

"Look at the steep sides of those mountains," marveled Barnaby as the adventurers took in their surroundings. "It looks like we're in a valley, except that it's filled with water!"

"When the clue said 'cruise,' I thought it would be like Montego Bay," said Babette, a hint of disappointment in her voice. "But it is much cooler here."

"That's because we're at 61 degrees north latitude," offered Beauregard. "Let's look on the map and see exactly where we are this time."

"Here we are," said Bridget, pointing to the map. "We're in northern Europe, near the coast across the North Sea from Great Britain. This coastline has lots of inlets, making it quite ragged."

"Oh, look!" Babette exclaimed, pointing to one side of the waterway where a waterfall tumbled hundreds of feet down the mountain into the water. "That is so beautiful!"

"What does the guidebook say about this area?" said Barnaby.

"It says we're on the coast of Norway," Bridget began, after thumbing through several sections. "And this waterway is called a **fjord**, a steep-walled, narrow inlet 'valley' that penetrates a coastal waterway. Fjords are found all along this coastline, but this one is the largest. It's called the Sonje Fjord."

Mountains

Mountains

Water

Figure 35: Fjord

"Is this the only place in the world that has fjords?" inquired Babette, thinking that she would like to visit others someday if all fjords were as lovely as this.

"No," responded Bridget, after consulting the guidebook some more. "Fjords are also found on the coast of Alaska, the southwestern coast of South America, and on the edge of Antarctica."

"The fjord is so narrow," began Barnaby. "It must be difficult to navigate the ship along it. I wonder if it's also shallow."

"Not according to the information here," Bridget replied. "It says that the water in a fjord can be quite deep. One in this area is 4,000 feet deep and another, along Antarctica's coast, is 6,000 feet deep!"

"Four thousand feet deep!" remarked Barnaby as he looked over the railing at the water.

"Yes," continued Bridget. "The fjords were formed by the erosion of glaciers, but some scientists think that movement of the earth's plates may have contributed to their depth."

The discussion about the depth of the water made Beauregard a little apprehensive. "These three sure have a knack of getting into dangerous situations," he thought. "And I don't relish the idea of saving them from the depths if they fall overboard or the ship sinks."

In order to be prepared for any possibility, Beauregard began to walk around the deck in search of life preservers. Not far from where the four friends had been standing, he saw a large box bolted to the deck labeled "Life Preservers." Beauregard opened the lid for a peek. To his shock, there was a metal cylinder, sitting on top of dozens of bright orange life preservers! He called the kids over to the box to view his find.

"Beauregard!" said Bridget as she put her arm around his shoulder. "You found this cylinder in record time. What would we do without you?"

"What, indeed!" thought Beauregard.

"So, let's open it up and get on with our search for the treasure," Barnaby interjected, reaching down for the cylinder.

You're getting closer and closer! BVM

Clue #17: 51 degrees north latitude and 1.5 degrees east longitude—You'll be in a tight spot, but go toward the white cliffs!

"One and a half degrees east longitude—we'll be near the prime meridian," noted Barnaby as he dialed the coordinates to continue their journey.

✍ EXERCISE #13 ✍
A Trip Down the Sonje Fjord

Pretend that your class is getting ready to go on a trip to Norway. Your flight has landed in Oslo, the capital, and you catch a commuter plane to Bergen, a fishing community along the coastline. As you board a bus and travel over high peaks and around hairpin curves, you reach the ferry that travels up the Sonje Fjord. When you return home, you are selected by the class to write an article about the trip for the school paper. Write the article, as descriptively as possible, so that your readers can visualize all aspects of the fjord.

✎ ✎ ✎ ✎ ✎

"Barnaby! You did it again!" yelled Bridget after she bobbed to the surface and began treading water.

"Sorry," Barnaby replied sheepishly. "But 'a tight spot' and 'cliffs' made me think we were heading to a ravine or something—not water!"

Beauregard, wishing he had one of those life preservers from the ship, swam with Babette over to the quarreling twosome. "Let's just get out of wherever we are instead of quibbling," he told Bridget and Barnaby, although he was a little more than peeved at being dunked again himself.

"I recognize this place!" announced Babette as she looked toward the shore. "We are in the Strait of Dover, located between Great Britain and the European mainland."

"A strait...connects two bodies of water...narrow...a tight place," Barnaby mumbled to himself, remembering their visit to the southern tip of South America.

"I came here with my family once—I'd recognize the White Cliffs of Dover anywhere," Babette continued as she indicated the shoreline's steep cliffs and milky appearance.

"The clue said to head toward the white cliffs, so let's do it," Bridget told the others.

The questers began swimming toward the gleaming cliffs on the shore, thankful for the day's calm water. Babette, a skilled swimmer, was soon leading the group. Her arms cut through the water in strong, practiced strokes. Nearing shore, her left arm struck an object in the water.

"Pollution!" was Babette's first thought on striking the object, which bobbed back up to the surface. Stopping to find out what some careless person had thrown in the water, Babette discovered a glass bottle, about a foot long, sealed with a large cork. Anchored in place with a chain, the bottle contained a piece of paper. Babette waited for her friends to swim closer before calling out to them.

"Maybe I have found a message from a shipwreck," she suggested to the others as they looked at the bottle. "It is not a cylinder, but it may be interesting to read what is inside when we reach the shore."

The questers released the bottle from its anchor, and Babette held on to it as she started off toward shore again. When they reached the shore and found a place to rest, the adventurers opened the bottle and read the note.

Sorry to confuse you, but a cylinder would sink! This is your last clue—good luck as you return to the western hemisphere! BVM

Clue #18: 40 degrees north latitude and 4 degrees west longitude—The table has water on three sides. Travel north to a big stone house.

"The last clue," gasped Babette. "Do you think this one will lead us to the treasure?"

"Well, we'll be returning to the western hemisphere," noted Barnaby. "And that means we have just about traveled around the entire world."

"Let's look on the map to see where the coordinates are located," Bridget interjected.

"I wonder what a table with water on three sides means," said Barnaby.

Beauregard held the map as the questers determined that the latitude and longitude designations would take them to the Iberian Peninsula in Europe. Anticipating a need for more information, Babette pulled the guidebook out of the backpack.

"What does it say?" inquired Bridget eagerly.

"It says that a **peninsula** is a land mass surrounded by water on three sides," Babette informed them. "Europe has many peninsulas. For its size, Europe has a longer coastline than any other continent, and this is primarily due to the many peninsulas."

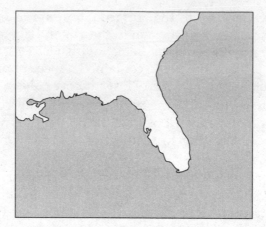

Figure 36: Peninsula

"Many of the great sailors who explored the earth hundreds of years ago, such as Magellan and Columbus, came from Europe," Barnaby added. "Maybe this area produced so many sailors because it has a long coastline and a lot of seaports."

"That sounds logical," said Bridget. "But how are tables related to peninsulas?"

"Maybe it means the Iberian Peninsula rather than just any peninsula," Beauregard suggested. "See what the guidebook says about the Iberian Peninsula, Babette."

"Good point!" Babette said as she began to look for the information. "It says the Atlantic Ocean and Mediterranean Sea are on the west and east, with the Strait of Gibraltar connecting the two bodies of water to the south. A mountain range stands on the northern side of the peninsula where it connects with the rest of the European continent, and there is a large, flat area, called the Meseta Plateau, on the peninsula itself."

"Flat?" Barnaby interrupted. "A table is flat. What does it say about plateaus?"

Babette soon found the next topic and read: "A **plateau** is an area of high, flat land which may be rather small or cover much of a continent. Africa is primarily a plateau that is bordered by a coastal lowland. Plateaus are also called tablelands."

"Tablelands!" exclaimed Barnaby. "That's got to be the meaning of that part of the clue. We have to travel north on the Meseta Plateau!"

"And how many old stone houses do you think we will find in an area that has been inhabited for so long?" added Bridget, feeling a little discouraged. "Probably zillions."

✍ EXERCISE #14 ✐
Peninsulas, Plateaus, and Other Flat Things

From details in this chapter and from any other references, describe the similarities and differences between a **peninsula**, a **plateau,** and an **isthmus**. Prepare a drawing to support your analysis.

Chapter 11
Finding the Treasure

After dialing the latest clue, the questers found themselves standing on an expanse of dry, flat land. They soaked in the warmth of the sun after their swim in the Strait of Dover. A dusty road stretched into the distance, and a few houses dotted the landscape.

"Let's determine the direction of north from this point," suggested Barnaby as he pulled the compass out of the backpack. "We have to travel north, remember?"

Bridget, Barnaby, Babette, and Beauregard faced north and began walking along the road, exchanging greetings with fellow travelers and farmers along the way. As they passed one of the old stone houses, a woman came out and offered the four friends water, which quenched their thirst. It was hot work walking along the dry, dusty road.

The small road finally joined another, larger road, that also headed north. After walking along the larger road for a few minutes, the group came upon a bus of tourists which had been heading south before mechanical problems halted its progress. The tourists, looking displeased that their sightseeing was being delayed, sat under a nearby group of trees as the driver peered at the engine.

"Can we help?" offered Bridget as the questers approached the driver, who was now tapping at the engine with a wrench.

"I wish you could," replied the driver, "but I'm afraid this is going to take a mechanic. You haven't seen a place with a telephone within the last few miles, have you?"

"There was a store a few miles down the small road we were on," Babette said. "It might have had a telephone."

"I've never been down that side road," said the driver with a grateful smile. "Sounds like it might be worth a try..."

"Have you been here long?" asked Beauregard as he eyed the restless tourists.

"Not too long, but tourists are usually impatient," the bus driver noted. "I told my boss that this bus was overdue for a maintenance check and shouldn't be sent way out to that old castle. He'll be the one who'll have to answer to these tourists!"

"What old castle?" asked Bridget. She had never seen a real castle, and was intrigued by the thought.

"It's about two miles north of here," replied the driver. "People visit it frequently because many famous people from this area have lived there. It's in good shape for such an old structure. I guess they built things to last in those days."

At the words "old" and "stone" the four explorers pricked up their ears.

"If someone lived there, even if it was a long time ago, it's still a house," reasoned Barnaby.

"And it is old and made of stone," Babette added.

"Let's go see what we can find," suggested Beauregard, who was getting restless standing around the bus.

Bridget, Barnaby, Babette, and Beauregard wished the bus driver good luck and walked quickly along the road. The driver had mentioned that the castle tours ended in the late afternoon.

After walking the couple of miles, a stone structure came into view to the questers' left. While the building lacked the high, pointed towers of castles in fairy tales, it was nevertheless an impressive structure on the landscape. At the gate, the questers gained admission for the last tour and set out for the entrance to the building.

The tour guide seemed relieved that she only had four guests on her last tour—it had been a busy day. She showed the adventurers around the castle, from the great dining hall to the dungeon, as she told them about the famous people who had lived there. The tour was extremely interesting, but the questers didn't see anything that would lead them to think the treasure could be in this old stone building.

"Do you know anyone at the United Nations?" Bridget asked

the tour guide hopefully as they descended the staircase back toward the entrance.

"No, dear. I don't!" laughed the guide as she smiled at Bridget with a puzzled expression. "Why do you ask?"

"Oh, no reason really," Bridget responded, a little embarrassed. "You just get a lot of visitors here, I guess."

The tour ended and the guide pointed the guests in the direction of the exit. She wished them a good afternoon before she went back upstairs to prepare the castle for closing.

"Struck out again!" sighed Barnaby as he shrugged his shoulders. "We'll just have to keep looking, I suppose."

"Do you think we missed something in the clue?" Bridget asked her friends.

Before any of them could answer, a strangely familiar voice from behind the staircase said, "No, actually, you have arrived at the correct location."

Bridget, Barnaby, Babette, and Beauregard whirled around to see an old man with a long gray beard step out from behind the staircase.

"Silas Filmore!" Bridget exclaimed as she recognized the old man who had given them the guidebook and Coordinator. "What are you doing here?"

Silas chuckled softly as he observed the slack-jawed surprise on the questers' faces. He stepped forward, pausing briefly to reach under a table and lift up a small chest.

"I'm here to give you the treasure Bartholomew Van Morrow promised if you completed the mission, of course!" Silas replied. "You were rather resourceful during your mission, too, I might add!"

"So it was you?" Babette asked, surprise and disbelief in her voice. "I felt like someone was shadowing us, but I never dreamed it would be you!"

"It was me, all right!" replied Silas with a grin. "I hope I didn't scare you, but I wanted to make sure you were learning the geography skills and knowledge that my old friend Bartholomew would have desired."

"You knew Mr. Van Morrow?" inquired Barnaby.

"Oh, yes," nodded Silas. "Bartholomew Van Morrow and I knew

each other for many years and traveled all over the world together. In fact, I rather enjoyed the travels you four experienced because it reminded me of the old days with Bartholomew. Of course, the places also reminded me how much I miss my dear friend."

Silas, saddened as he thought of his old companion, paused for a few seconds before he held the chest out to the questers, saying, "Here you go—a treasure worth $20 million for UNICEF! Go ahead, open it!"

The four friends approached the chest and slowly lifted the lid. Inside was a set of maps...very old maps. The paper on which they were drawn had yellowed with age, but it was obvious that the maps had been drawn with meticulous care. In the corner of each one was the signature "C. Columbus."

"C. Columbus," read Barnaby incredulously. "The real Christopher Columbus?"

"Yes, that's right." Silas nodded his head and smiled. "These are the original maps drawn by Christopher Columbus when he returned to Europe after his famous voyage to the New World in 1492. A fitting treasure for a group of young people who have also made discoveries about the world's geography."

Under the maps, there was a letter from Bartholomew Van Morrow. A flush of pride and accomplishment came across the explorers' faces as they read the letter congratulating them on successfully completing their mission by utilizing a knowledge of geography, and for helping the world's needy children in such a great way.

"What do we do now?" asked Bridget, suddenly feeling at a loss for something to do.

"Go back to New York, of course!" answered Silas Filmore. "You still have the Coordinator, don't you?"

Like the knowledgeable individuals they were, the questers utilized their skills in geography to determine the coordinates of New York City and set the Coordinator's dials. Bridget, Barnaby, Babette, Beauregard, and Silas Filmore gathered around the machine to return to the place the adventure had begun.

Chapter 12
Handing Over
the Check!

The five travelers found themselves back on the sidewalk in New York City from which they had departed. The subway entrance was down the street and Silas Filmore's apartment was nearby. As Bridget, Barnaby, Babette, and Beauregard looked around as if to make sure they weren't dreaming, a limousine screeched to a halt in front of them. Somewhat surprised, the friends watched as the uniformed driver with the long face got out and came around to the other side of the limousine to open the door for them.

"Let me introduce Mr. Robert Ewing," Silas Filmore said. "Mr. Ewing served as Mr. Van Morrow's private chauffeur for many years."

Mr. Ewing nodded a formal greeting as the group entered the limousine. There was more than enough room for the five passengers as they stretched out on its comfortable seats.

"Where are we going?" queried Barnaby.

"Why, to the United Nations, of course! There are dignitaries awaiting our arrival," Silas informed Barnaby. "You four are the toast of the town for earning a $20 million donation for UNICEF!"

Bridget, Babette, Barnaby, and Beauregard stared at the cheering crowd awaiting their arrival outside the United Nations building. They smiled and waved a little self-consciously as they walked up the red carpet that led from the limousine to the main entrance. Once inside, they were escorted into a large room where delegates from all over the world were gathered for the presentation ceremony.

"Mom!" Bridget exclaimed as she saw her mother standing near the steps as the group was being led to the stage. "What are you doing here?"

"Being very proud of the accomplishments of my daughter and her friends," her mother said, beaming at Bridget and the others.

The ceremony began with a speech about the importance of UNICEF's work for the children of the world, and how the $20 million dollars could be used to help them. It ended with Bridget, Barnaby, Babette, and Beauregard holding a large check. The check, made out to UNICEF for $20 million, was presented to the UNICEF director by the four friends as hundreds of camera flashes recorded the event. The presentation was followed by a reception during which the questers were congratulated over and over again by many important people.

"I was worried during our trip that we wouldn't meet our deadline," Bridget told Barnaby, Babette, and Beauregard when they got a few minutes to themselves. "But look at the date on the calendar—we finished with weeks to spare!"

"What excellent timing, Bridget," said her mother, walking up to the group. "My friend called the other day and said that there was still room at Camp Novachuk for a couple of weeks this month. What about it—want to go?"

Bridget turned her panic-stricken face to her friends and whispered, "Guys, we've got to find another adventure—FAST!"

✍ EXERCISE #15 ✍
Hide Treasures from Your Friends

Design several quests for your classmates. Select treasures or places on the earth for them to find. You can hide treasures on mountain tops or on the banks of rivers. Develop clues composed of coordinates of longitude and latitude as well as other physical geography concepts. Use the illustrations in this book and any other reference materials you can find. And yes, you can use the Coordinator.

Start out like this:

Clue #1   Go to North America and sit on the Golden Gate Bridge in the San Francisco Bay.

Clue #2   Use the Coordinator and dial the following: 38^0 N latitude and 122^0 W longitude.

Glossary

MAJOR GEOGRAPHICAL TERMS

absolute location
the exact point where two lines intersect; a point where latitude and longitude intersect or cross each other

altitude
the height of a point on earth above sea level

anthropology
the study of human beings and their cultural classifications, such as physical characteristics and social relations

archipelago
a group of islands or an area of water that contains many islands

archeology
the scientific study of the remains of various cultures

artesian water
water from a well that is created by internal pressure in the earth; it flows up like a fountain

atlas
a bound collection of maps, records, and statistics about the earth

atoll
a circular coral island that encloses a lagoon

bay
a body of water that penetrates a coastline

brook
a small body of water that flows into a larger body of water

cape
a small point of land, surrounded by water on three sides, which extends into the sea

coral reef
a collection of coral—the skeletons of small creatures called polyps—which accumulates under the water's surface; coral can accumulate to a height which pushes above the water's surface to form an island

channel
water that runs in a depression cut in loose soil or solid rock; also known as a river bed; a channel can also be a passage of water connecting two larger bodies of water

climate
an area's average weather over a long period of time, which is influenced by many factors

continental divide
a point on the mountains of a continent that determines the direction a river will flow

continent
one of the seven great divisions of land on the earth

Coriolis force
a deflecting force on the earth due to the earth's rotation

cyclone
a violent ocean windstorm in the Indian Ocean

delta
triangular-shaped land found at the mouth of some large rivers; soil is transported by the river in such large amounts that coastal waters cannot carry it all away

desert
an area or region that receives less than 10 inches of precipitation per year

equator
zero degrees latitude that divides the earth in half, into the northern hemisphere and the southern hemisphere

faults
the earth is covered with an outer covering much like an egg shell; this thick covering is divided into large pieces, much like a jigsaw puzzle is divided into connecting pieces. These pieces are called plates, and the lines where these plates make contact are called faults. Faults influence the formation of mountains and rift valleys.

flood
where excess rain water rises above the river banks and pours over onto the land

geography
the science of the physical and cultural characteristics of the earth

glacier
huge sheets of ice that are in motion; soil erosion from glaciers causes depressions in the soil or rock along its trail

gulf
part of a sea or ocean that is partially enclosed by a coastline

hemisphere
one-half of the earth divided either at the equator or from pole to pole

hurricane
a violent windstorm in the Atlantic Ocean

ice shelf
a huge glacier

international date line
the point at which one day ends and another begins

island
a body of land completely surrounded by water

isthmus
a narrow strip of land with water on both sides

latitude
parallel lines that run north and south to help measure points on earth

lake
an inland body of water that is surrounded by land on all sides

lagoon
a small body of water that is separated from the rest of the ocean

longitude
lines that run east and west to help measure points on earth; also called **meridians**

ocean currents
underwater rivers that direct water from one part of the ocean to another

ocean
one of the four largest bodies of water that covers nearly three-fourths of the earth

outlet
an opening in a lake where streams take water to a river

peninsula
a land mass surrounded by water on three sides

pole
zero degrees north latitude or south latitude; an imaginary highest point north and south of the equator

plain
a broad, flat expanse of land

plateau
an area of high, flat land which may be small or may cover much of a continent

prime meridian
zero degrees longitude; runs from the North Pole to the South Pole; when connected with the international date line, divides the earth into the eastern and western hemispheres

quadrant
one of four parts; one-fourth

rain forest
thick growth of trees with the tallest trees reaching more than 200 feet tall; underneath the tall trees are shorter trees and thick vegetation

relative location
a general location; for example, the Empire State Building is in New York City

rift valley
a narrow valley created by two earth plates moving away from a fault line

river
a natural stream with increasing volumes of water, usually beginning near mountain tops

river basin

the beginning points of several rivers and all their tributaries, which can be connected at all points to form a basin area

river bed

water in a river travels in a depression; also known as a channel

savanna

an area in tropical or subtropical zones of the world that borders or surrounds rain forests

sea

a large body of water that may be composed of salt water or fresh water; may be landlocked

sea level

the average height of the world's oceans

steppe

often called grassland; found in subtropical or temperate regions that border interior deserts

strait

a very narrow passage of water that connects two larger bodies of water

stream

a small body of water that may feed into a lake

typhoon

a violent ocean windstorm in the Pacific Ocean

tributary

a small running stream of water that flows into a larger river

weather

the daily state of the atmosphere with respect to hot or cold and wet or dry

Answers

Quiz #1
Quadrants

1. North America
2. Southeastern
3. Southwestern
4. Southwestern and south-eastern
5. Africa
6. Northwestern and south-western
7. Northeastern
8. Pacific
9. Pacific
10. Northeastern

Quiz #2
Longitude and Latitude

1. Atlantic Ocean
2. Pacific Ocean
3. Antarctica
4. Asia
5. Australia
6. South America
7. Europe
8. Africa
9. Arctic Ocean
10. Indian Ocean

Quiz #3
True or False

1. True
2. False
3. True
4. True
5. True
6. True
7. True
8. True
9. True
10. True
11. False
12. False

Quiz #4
Checking Out Rain Forests

1. 200 feet
2. Animals, birds, and insects
3. Two-thirds
4. Special medicinal properties
5. Earth's lungs, oxygen
6. Ten tons
7. 6 percent, 50 million
8. Decreases
9. Pollution
10. Global warming, polar

11. Nutrient
12. Crops
13. Decaying leaves
14. Abandoned
15. Populations, raw materials, mineral

Quiz #5
Search and Find

1. North America, South American, Asia, Africa, Australia (Most geographers include the numerous islands in the South Pacific area as Oceania. Some geographers include Australia and New Zealand and the numerous islands that stretch for 8,000 miles as Oceania.)
2. South America and Africa
3. The Amazon Basin

Quiz #6
Trace the River Basins

1. An area from the beginning of the river and all its tributaries that is connected by those points to form the shape and size of the basin.
2. Amazon, Vaupes, Japura, Tapajos
3. Uruguay, Paraguay, and Parana Rivers
4. Hint: Look first at a physical map of the United States in an atlas.
5. The Amazon carries the highest volume of water. The Nile is the longest river.

Quiz #7
A Mixed Bag

1. Temperature drops with altitude.
2. It is the highest navigable lake in the world.
3. It means that Jones City is 582 feet above sea level.
4. Mathematically, about 20 degrees; however, this is not close to the average temperature of Denver, which is about 50 degrees. Obviously, there are many more factors that influence weather.

Quiz #8
Channels, Straits, and Capes

1. c
2. b
3. d
4. a

Quiz #9
True or False

1. True
2. False
3. True
4. True
5. True
6. True
7. True
8. True
9. True
10. True
11. True

12. True
13. True
14. True
15. True
16. True
17 True
18. False
19. True
20. True

Quiz #10
Time Zones

1. 7 a.m., North America
2. 1 p.m., Europe
3. 1 a.m., North America
4. 5 a.m., North America
5. 7 p.m., Asia
6. 4 p.m., North America
7. 2 a.m., Pacific Ocean
8. 1 p.m., Europe
9. 3 p.m., Africa
10. 9 p.m., Asia
11. 12 noon, Africa
12. 8 a.m., South America
13. 4 a.m., North America
14. 1 p.m., Europe
15. 8 p.m., Asia
16. 10 p.m., Australia
17. 7 p.m., Asia
18. 2 p.m., Africa
19. 3 p.m., Europe
20. 9 a.m., South America

Quiz #11
Climate and Weather

1. The Ganges and Brahmaputra.

2. Deltas are formed when sediment carried in the river is deposited at the end of the river as it flows into the ocean.

3. Monsoon winds bring moisture and warmth from ocean regions near the equator. Cooling as they pass over land, the moisture is deposited as heavy rain.

4. The air over tropical seas is warm. As it rises it is cooled and storm clouds are formed. The winds add to the storm activity.

5. Weather refers to the condition day to day—rain, sunshine, etc. Climate refers to an area's average weather over a long period of time, for example, months, years, or decades.

6. As air cools as it rises on the windward side of the mountain, it loses its moisture (rainfall, snow, etc.). There is little moisture left once the air gets over to the other (leeward) side of the mountain.

7. The greenhouse effect is a warming of our global temperature by a build-up of pollutants. Limiting the use of pollutants such as carbon monoxide, aerosol sprays, etc. can help.

Quiz #12
Checking Out Mountains

1. Volcanic mountains are formed when melted rock, formed by the heat of friction that results from plates rubbing together, pushes up out of the earth.

2. Inactive volcanoes no longer contain molted rock; these mountains do not erupt, or spew molten lava.

3. Everest, Asia
   Cerro Aconcagua, South America
   McKinley, North America
   Kilimanjaro, Africa
   Vinson Massif, Antarctica
   Kazeb, Europe
   Kosciusko, Australia
   Everest—29,028 ft
   Godwin-Austen—28,250 ft
   Kanchenjunga—28,208 ft
   Lhotse—27,923 ft
   Makalu—27,824 ft

4. The Rocky Mountains are not as old geologically as the Appalachian Mountains, which have been worn down over time by the elements.

5. Some of the highest mountains are under the ocean.

6. Double check your responses!

7. 29,028 subtract 20,320 = 8,708 ft higher.

8. Everest 29,028 ft divided by yards (3 ft in one yard) = 9,676 yards.

9. Everest 29,028 ft divided by 5,280 ft = 5.5 miles high.

10. McKinley 20,320 ft at the rate of 10 feet per minute = 2,032 minutes or 34 hours.

Quiz #13
Permafrost and the Tundra

1. Permafrost remains all year. In the summer, the temperature rises to approximately 50 degrees Fahrenheit. The top few inches of soil may thaw enough to support some vegetation. In the winter, the temperature falls to minus 40 degrees Fahrenheit.

2. Approximately 67 degrees north latitude.

3. There is no land farther enough south to qualify as tundra.

Quiz #14
Checking Out Deserts and Seas

1. They are the boundaries for the tropic zone.

2. Subtropical deserts can get very hot during the day but temperatures drop quickly as night. These deserts usually occur on the western half of a continent.

   Interior deserts can be found in temperate climates. These are usually in the middle of a continent.

Coastal deserts are usually found in the southern hemisphere and lose their moisture before reaching land.

Polar deserts are extremely cold; the air in these regions is too cold to retain any moisture.

3. A sea is a small body of water that lies along the margins of an ocean. The Caribbean Sea is the largest and deepest of all the seas.

4. The Dead Sea has no outlets and all of the salt remains. It contains no signs of life. The saltwater contains much more salt than the oceans.

5. The major seas are as follows: Caribbean, Mediterranean, Bering, Sea of Okhotsk, East China Sea, Sea of Japan, North Sea, Black Sea, Red Sea, and Baltic Sea.

Quiz #15
True or False

1. True
2. True
3. True
4. True
5. False
6. False
7. True
8. True
9. True
10. True
11. True
12. True
13. False
14. False
15. False

Quiz #16
Time to Review

1. The topography of the land is so different on either side of the mountains.

2. Somewhat similar.

3. 30 yards; 3/10 of the length of a football field.

4. Yes

5. Altitude is going up, in height. It is opposite of below.

Exercise #1
Using an Atlas

1. Parallels become shorter as they approach the poles.

2. Asia, Africa, North America, South America, Antarctica, Europe, and Australia.

3. Pacific—64,186, 000; 36, 198
   Atlantic—31,862, 000; 28, 198
   Indian—28,350, 000; 25, 344
   Arctic—5,427, 000; 17, 880

Exercise #2
Rivers, Lakes, and Oceans

1. St. Lawrence River

2. Mississippi, Missouri, and Ohio

3. Superior, Huron, Michigan, Erie, and Ontario

4. Orinoco, Atlantic
   Amazon, Atlantic
   Uruguay, Atlantic
   Paraguay, Atlantic
   Parana, Atlantic

5. Indian Ocean. The Ganges is special because it is the sacred river of the Hindus.

Exercise #3
Rivers and Canyons

1. It is located on the eastern edge of the continent along the Great Dividing Range.

2. Hydroelectric power for electricity.

3. Rivers are used for transportation, irrigation, and recreation.

4. Suggestion: Begin with the Grand Canyon in North America (Arizona, USA).

5. Hint: Visit a new home construction site before grass has been sewn and observe what happens after a heavy rain.

Exercise #4
Review

1. Volcanic action and coral deposits.

2. Yes, an archipelago is a group of islands located in proximity of each other.

3. A gulf is much larger than a bay but they both penetrate a coastline.

4. Coral forms an island by the process of accumulation

until it pushes above the water's surface.

5. The lagoon is separated from the rest of the ocean.

6. The North Equatorial and Canary Currents propelled his ship in a southwestern direction from Spain.

7. Wind, water, temperature, earth's rotation.

8. The rotation of the earth causes the Coriolis force. The currents travel clockwise in the northern hemisphere and counter-clockwise in the southern hemisphere.

9. The storms in the Atlantic are called hurricanes and storms in the Pacific are called typhoons.

10. Warm water from the equator is propelled by the trade winds until it intersects land and it is deflected northward.

Exercise #5
A Scavenger Hunt...Are You Game?

1. 2 degrees south latitude and 118 degrees east longitude

2. 20 degrees south latitude and 40 degrees east longitude

3. 3 degrees south latitude and 108 degrees east longitude

4. 35 degrees south latitude and 118 degrees east longitude

5. 4 degrees south latitude and 52 degrees east longitude

6. 67 degrees north latitude and 57 degrees west longitude

7. 62 degrees north latitude and 72 degrees west longitude

8. 42 degrees north latitude and 70 degrees west longitude

9. 22 degrees north latitude and 86 degrees west longitude

10. 35 degrees north latitude and 75 degrees west longitude

11. 53 degrees south latitude and 70 degrees west longitude

12. 55 degrees south latitude and 68 degrees west longitude

13. 15 degrees south latitude and 142 degrees west longitude

14. 53 degrees south latitude and 68 degrees west longitude

15. 5 degrees south latitude and 35 degrees west longitude

16. 50 degrees north latitude and 3 degrees west longitude

17. 36 degrees north latitude and 7 degrees west longitude

18. 52 degrees north latitude and 6 degrees west longitude

19. 38 degrees north latitude and 16 degrees east longitude

20. 40 degrees north latitude and 19 degrees east longitude

21. 65 degrees north latitude and 170 degrees west longitude

22. 20 degrees north latitude and 108 degrees east longitude

23. 10 degrees north latitude and 79 degrees east longitude

24. 27 degrees north latitude and 57 degrees east longitude

25. 24 degrees north latitude and 118 degrees east longitude

26. 18 degrees north latitude and 17 degrees west longitude

Exercise #6
A Trip to the South Pole

1. You may list things such as shelter, food, communication devices, etc.

2. You may have to experiment with this a few times before you get it right.

Exercise #7
Learning About the Land Down Under

1. Scuba diving and snorkeling allows you to see the many colorful and interesting sea animals and fish around the coral reef. The Caribbean Sea also has coral reefs.

2. Hint: Call a travel agent and get some ideas and perhaps literature from them.

3. Australia is almost 3 million square miles; New Zealand a little over 100,000 square miles. Australia is mostly dry and hot; New Zealand is mild and has more rainfall. Australia is a continent; New Zealand is composed of two islands. Australia has much land covered with semi-desert scrub plant life; New Zealand has lush pasture land. Australia is mostly flat land; New Zealand is mainly mountainous.

4. The Indian Ocean.

Exercise #8
Globetrotters' Challenges

1. First you would determine how many miles there are in each time zone: 69 miles x 15 degrees =1,035 miles. Now you know there are 24 time zones (24 x 1035) = 24,840.

The actual mileage is 24,902 miles.

2. No, the distance within a particular time zone may narrow as the degrees of latitude become shorter.

Exercise #9
Checking Out Rocks

1. Ayers Rock is a large sandstone rock that got its shape after the mass of sandstone in the area was worn down by wind and rain.

2. The three major types of rocks are igneous, sedimentary, and metamorphic. Igneous rocks form from volcanic magma or lava after it cools. The most common types of sedimentary rocks are broken into particles of sediment by water, ice, and wind. Sediments are carried to lakes and oceans where they accumulate for thousands of years. In time, the weight of continuous sediment deposits forces downward and hardens or cements the bottom layers into sedimentary rocks. Metamorphic rocks form when other types of rocks are pushed down inside the earth and are changed by heat and pressure over thousands of years.

3. The Himalayas were once part of the sea floor. Almost 50 million years ago, the Indian plate crashed into the Asian plate and pushed up the highest mountain range in the world.

4. The Rocky Mountains are young mountains with jagged and pointed rock. The Appalachian Mountains are millions of years old, and have been worn down by the forces of nature.

Exercise #10
The Weather

1. Talk with your teacher to find out what materials you will need for your presentation. Use some time to plan the role of each presenter.

2. Make sure you get proper video equipment and that you have maps that you can mark on. You could laminate the maps and use water color markers (which can be erased) to mark on them.

Exercise #11
Library Activity

1. 23.5 degrees
2. The dry air of the desert doesn't retain heat once the sun sets.

Exercise #12
Cleopatra's Nile

1. Lake Victoria
2. They were used as burial sites or tombs.
3. What did you learn about Cleopatra?
4. Share your drawing with your parents and teachers.

Exercise #13
A Trip Down the Sonje Fjord

As you land in Oslo, describe what you see when you get off the plane (e.g. land forms). Continue your description of Norway as you head toward Bergen. You may want to describe how the city of Bergen compares with the city of Oslo. Be very specific about your bus trip to the Sonje Fjord. Complete your article by describing what you see from the boat as you travel down the fjord. Be sure to describe the calm water, the mountains, the many beautiful waterfalls, and the excitement you felt as you entered the open ocean.

Exercise #14
Peninsulas, Plateaus, and Other Flat Things

A peninsula is a land mass surrounded by water on three sides. A plateau is an area of high flat land which may be rather small or can cover much of a continent.

An isthmus is a narrow strip of land with water on both sides. Suggestion on the drawing: Check out the country of Spain and the state of Florida when looking at peninsulas. Also look at Africa as a plateau, and follow North America until it reaches South America to find an isthmus.

Exercise #15
Hide Treasures from Your Friends

Have fun with Geography!

ABOUT THE AUTHOR

Dr. J. Allen Queen is a former classroom teacher and school principal. He is presently a professor in the Department of Middle, Secondary and K-12 Education at the University of North Carolina in Charlotte, NC.

Dr. Queen is an active member of the National Council for the Social Studies and serves as the editor of *Inquiry in Social Studies: Curriculum, Research and Instruction*, the journal of the North Carolina Council for the Social Studies. Dr. Queen's hobbies include karate, on which he has written nine books, and watching his son, Alex, grow and learn about the wonderful world in which we live.

More Bestselling Smart Junior Titles from The Princeton Review

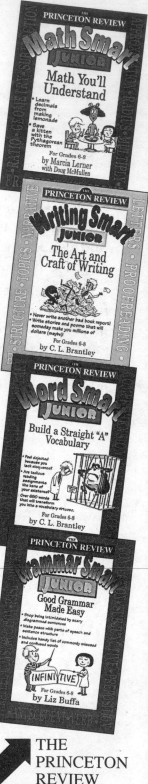

A 1995 Parents Choice Gold Medal Award-Winning Series

Join Barnaby, Babette, Bridget, their fat cat friend Beauregard, and all the crazy people they meet as they travel around the world, across time, and through space in search of adventure and knowledge.

"Educational and entertaining describes this series. The Princeton Review has made learning just plain fun."

—*Writing Teacher* magazine

AMERICAN HISTORY SMART JUNIOR
$12.00 • 0-679-77357-6
A time travel adventure through history!

ASTRONOMY SMART JUNIOR
$12.00 • 0-679-76906-4
Blast off to Mars with the Smart Junior gang.

GEOGRAPHY SMART JUNIOR
$12.00 • 0-679-77522-6
The Smart Junior gang has to solve a mystery by finding clues from all over the world.

GRAMMAR SMART JUNIOR
$12.00 • 0-679-76212-4
Good grammar made easy. Selected by *Curriculum Administrator* magazine readers as one of the Top 100 Products of 1995-96.

MATH SMART JUNIOR
$12.00 • 0-679-75935-2
Save a kitten with the Pythagorean theorem and more! "Learning at its giggliest," says the *Chicago Tribune KIDNEWS*.

WORD SMART JUNIOR
$12.00 • 0-679-75936-0
Build a straight A vocabulary with the Smart Junior gang as they have a crazy adventure with over 650 vocabulary words.

WRITING SMART JUNIOR
$12.00 • 0-679-76131-4
Book reports, school papers, letter writing, story writing and even poetry are covered in *Writing Smart Junior*, selected by The New York Public Library for its 1996 Books for the Teen Age List.

THE
PRINCETON
REVIEW